HOW TO SURVIVE AN IRS ATTACK

Cheryl R. Frank, C.P.A., J.D.,
LL. M. in Taxation

KENDALL/HUNT PUBLISHING COMPANY
4050 Westmark Drive   Dubuque, Iowa 52002

Printed in the United States of America
10 9 8 7 6 5 4 3 2

Table of Contents

Part One
23 Tips for Surviving an IRS Audit

SURVIVAL STRATEGY #1

It is Important to Know Who You Are Dealing With Because the Individual Representative of the IRS May or May Not Have the Power or Authority to Grant the Relief You Are Seeking. Know Where to Go and Who to Call Within the IRS and Go Directly There.

SURVIVAL STRATEGY #2

Never, Never, Never Ignore an IRS Notice!!!

SURVIVAL STRATEGY #3

Do Not Attend an Audit Unprepared . . . Or Else!

SURVIVAL STRATEGY #4

Schedule the Audit Conference so That You Will Have Adequate Time to Compile Your Records. Do Not Be Intimidated into Submitting Information Which is Incomplete.

SURVIVAL STRATEGY #5

Compile and Organize Your Records Before the Audit. The First Step in Winning the Attack by the IRS is to Present Proof of Your Income and Deductions in a Way That Will Satisfy the Revenue Agent.

SURVIVAL STRATEGY #6

SURVIVAL STRATEGY #7

SURVIVAL STRATEGY #8

SURVIVAL STRATEGY #9

SURVIVAL STRATEGY #10

SURVIVAL STRATEGY #11

SURVIVAL STRATEGY #12

SURVIVAL STRATEGY #13

SURVIVAL STRATEGY #14

SURVIVAL STRATEGY #15

SURVIVAL STRATEGY #16

SURVIVAL STRATEGY #17

SURVIVAL STRATEGY #18

SURVIVAL STRATEGY #19

Part Two

8 Tips for Winning Your Case After Audit

Part Three

What Can You Do if You Can Not Afford to Pay the IRS?
9 Tips to Survive the IRS Attempt to Collect Taxes
When You Can Not Afford to Pay.

Preface

I first began my career as an attorney working for the Tax Litigation Division of the Office of Chief Counsel of the Internal Revenue Service. One of my responsibilities was to monitor and review cases in litigation to ascertain whether the case was being litigated in accordance with the policies of the Internal Revenue Service ("IRS"). After several months, I came to realize that a large percentage of the cases that came across my desk had been developed incorrectly by taxpayers.

The job of enforcement of the tax laws of our country is not black and white. In most cases, a taxpayer can win his case if there is a legal basis for the position that is taken and he can prove the facts necessary to substantiate his position. The IRS holds a taxpayer guilty until proven innocent. The taxpayer always has the burden of proof. I soon realized that taxpayers did not understand how to survive an audit or win their case in court. If they lost, taxpayers did not know how to minimize the impact of the collection process.

Through my training and experience at the IRS, I became an expert in IRS procedure. My background differs from the background of an IRS Revenue Agent or Revenue Officer. I was the person who saw the case at the end and I could evaluate the effectiveness of how the taxpayer had conducted their case. With this experience, I went to work with a major law firm where I had the opportunity to represent many taxpayers in their fight against the IRS. I did not win cases based solely on my knowledge of the tax law. I won cases by knowing how the IRS thinks. I knew how to use the system to achieve the most favorable outcome for my client.

In one of my first cases against the IRS, I was representing a taxpayer who had invested in a tax sheltered investment that I knew was on the IRS target list for litigation. My client was examined before many other taxpayers who made the same invest-ment. During the audit conference, I convinced the Revenue Agent that my client's case would be a bad case to proceed with because his facts differed from other investors and the IRS should be litigating the strongest cases first. I brought the taxpayer to the audit conference. He testified as he would have if the case went to court. The Revenue Agent could see what evidence I would present. At the audit level we were prepared to go all the way. The Revenue Agent concluded the audit without change. I believe that my client was one of the few investors in that particular tax shelter that was not assessed a deficiency. I was prepared and the Revenue Agent knew it. I could clearly distinguish our facts from the other cases. We won.

I assisted accountants and lawyers on major cases against the IRS. My approach was different from their approach and it was ef-fective for winning cases. Our technical knowledge of the tax law was the same. Our approach to winning cases was different.

I started writing articles for newspapers and magazines and I had the opportunity to give many speeches about how the IRS works. I met many people who had experiences in dealing with the IRS. What was common in all the stories I heard was that tax-payers were frustrated with the system. They had not been able to utilize the system to achieve a favorable outcome. I came in contact with taxpayers, rich and poor alike, who told the same story of how the IRS had taken control of their life, their assets, and their businesses, without reason. They all expressed fear of the IRS.

The majority of taxpayers can not afford tax lawyers to rep-resent them in dealing with the IRS. Accordingly, most people battle the IRS without the weapons necessary to win. Taxpayers are not generally aware of all of their rights and obligations. As a result, they do not know what questions to ask. They do not know how to win an audit or how to survive if they can not afford to pay their taxes. Other taxpayers expressed fear of coming back into the system if they had not filed their tax returns. Still others did not know where to go within the IRS if they could not resolve an issue. Without the necessary tools, the taxpayers recited similar stories of how their problems had magnified.

Many times, after I became involved, one or two phone calls to the right part of the IRS or a short letter alleviated the issue. Taxpayers would always tell me they had written letters for years with no result. I was not surprised since most of those letters went to the wrong division of the IRS. Most taxpayers did not understand the process to take to get matters resolved favorably. The IRS does publish many informational guides for taxpayers, but in many cases these guides are difficult for taxpayers to apply to their advantage.

As I started to speak publicly, the same issues repeated themselves. People are afraid of the IRS. Most taxpayers are law abiding and have a right to claim and defend all deductions they are entitled to. I felt I needed to write a simple book which non-attorneys could follow which answers many of the questions I have repeatedly been asked.

The IRS now estimates that there are ten million non-filers of tax returns. Each year approximately 1% of all tax returns are audited. During your lifetime, it is likely that you will come into contact with the IRS. Accordingly, everyone needs the knowledge to survive an IRS encounter. That is the purpose of this book. Remember . . . if all else fails, run, do not walk, to your nearest tax attorney or tax professional. As Judge Learned Hand once said ". . . you have no patriotic duty to pay more taxes than you owe. . . ."

Introduction

Former IRS Commissioner Jerome Kurtz once noted that there was a very high incentive for people to cheat on their taxes because the odds were against getting caught. Those odds are narrowing daily because of increased manpower and more sophisticated IRS computers. Clearly, one way to balance the federal deficit is to collect and assess taxes more efficiently.

Every year, more than a million Americans receive a chilling notice that the IRS wants to comb through their tax returns. The number of notices is increasing each year. It is not just the wealthy who face scrutiny. The IRS conducts tens of thousands of audits at random. Anyone can be the target.

To make matters worse, taxpayers always bear the burden of proof and are guilty until the tax return is proven to be accurate and complete as filed.

The IRS audits about one percent of all individual returns each year, though businesses and those in higher income brackets face added risk. The IRS also audits more than five percent of those individuals with income over $100,000. Even many who file simple tax returns are examined each year.

This is not surprising. The audit has become a major source of federal revenue. In one recent year, the IRS assessed more than $22 billion in additional taxes and penalties. In the following year, total assessments grew by almost 45%. That number is certain to increase with the pressure to balance the budget.

The penalties alone can be daunting. In one year, the IRS assessed more than 32 million taxpayers tax penalties. Fewer than 10 percent of those targeted succeeded in getting the penalties abated.

IRS computers identify those returns more likely to generate revenue on audit. The IRS may audit you if you have invested in a particular tax shelter that it has targeted. Many people are so afraid of IRS audits that the IRS estimates that nearly one in five taxpayers will fail to take advantage of legitimate deductions. Many other taxpayers are stumped by arcane tax forms. As the old joke goes, even Albert Einstein reportedly needed help on his tax return.

As complicated as the system seems, however, there are effective methods to deal with IRS audits.

If you receive an IRS notice, do not panic. You have not been selected because you are guilty or have been targeted for taking an illegal deduction. In many instances, the IRS computers generate a notice that identifies a discrepancy in the data that you reported.

More than 40 percent of all audits take place through the mail. If you receive a letter from the IRS asking you to mail in records needed to verify a specific item of income or deduction on your tax return, you should respond to this "correspondence audit" with the requested information in a timely manner. Remember, every IRS employee handles hundreds of cases. If you forward the requested information with a simple explanatory letter, the IRS will close your case quickly and in most cases, without change. In 21% of all audits, taxpayers receive a refund or no deficiency is found.

If you face an audit in person, you should present complete and accurate documentation. It is not the Revenue Agent's job to organize your records. If you are well prepared, however, you will be more likely to control the outcome of the audit. The IRS will not go away if you provide inadequate information.

Do not be afraid to take advantage of all available ways to save taxes. Keep accurate, complete and well-organized records. Remember: Your goal is to **win** the audit.

PART ONE

23 Tips for Surviving an IRS Audit

Strategies for Winning

SURVIVAL #1 STRATEGY

It is Important to Know Who You are Dealing With Because the Individual Representative of the IRS May or May Not Have the Power or Authority to Grant the Relief You Are Seeking. Know Where to Go and Who to Call Within the IRS and Go Directly There.

The organization of the IRS is important. A taxpayer must understand whom they are dealing with, what power that individual has, and how to protest an action by that person.

The IRS has four major functions:

◊ The IRS assists taxpayers in filing accurate returns and processing tax returns which are filed.

◊ The IRS determines tax due by auditing tax returns to make sure all taxpayers are complying with existing law.

◊ The IRS collects taxes from an estimated 20 million delinquent accounts and identifies the estimated 10 million taxpayers who have failed to file tax returns.

◊ The IRS conducts investigations, prosecutes cases and handles taxpayer appeals.

To guide IRS personnel in their daily activities, there is an "Internal Revenue Manual" that is a comprehensive manual setting forth the procedures for IRS personnel to comply with. It is one of the largest manuals of its kind. You should be aware that the IRS employee is bound by these IRS procedures. The Revenue Agent is also bound to follow IRS policies on legal issues. It is your responsibility as a taxpayer to protect your rights provided for under the law.

You may deal with one or more of the following individuals:

◊ Taxpayer Service Representatives—These individuals can answer your questions on how to prepare your tax return, which form to use or where to call for further assistance. These individuals can not work out collection agreements, hear your appeals or answer questions about your audit.

◊ Revenue Agents—These individuals are normally encountered during the audit. In auditing your tax return the Revenue Agent is bound by IRS policy and can not take into account the hazards of litigation. The job of the Revenue Agent is to verify the information you have reported on your tax return. Therefore, they can not consider whether your witness will provide credible testimony in court.

◊ Special Agents—These individuals investigate criminal tax matters. They have the power to execute and serve search and arrest warrants, issue subpoenas and summonses or seize property subject to forfeiture. **Run** to your nearest tax attorney if a Special Agent is involved in your case.

◊ Tax Law Specialists—These individuals are lawyers or CPA's who work in the National Office of the IRS in Washington, DC. They are experts in the law of a specialized area or industry. These individuals issue private letter rulings, answer technical advice requests or write IRS regulations.

◊ Revenue Officers—These individuals are charged with collecting delinquent taxes. They can seize your property without a court order, issue federal tax liens and levy your wages.

◊ Appeals Officers—These individuals have the power to review the audit report and negotiate a settlement with you. They can consider hazards of litigation and therefore have more latitude in negotiating a settlement than the Revenue Agent.

◊ District Counsel Attorneys—These individuals are charged with the job of litigating cases on behalf of the IRS when a taxpayer files a petition with the US Tax Court. They have the broadest discretion in negotiating a settlement.

It is important to remember whom you are dealing with because the individual may or may not have the authority to grant the relief you are seeking. In one instance, a taxpayer had come to me after writing many letters to the service center to place a hold on collection. The taxpayer should have contacted the Revenue Officer assigned to the case. Because the taxpayer did not contact the right party, the IRS kept levying taxpayer's bank accounts.

In other instances, many taxpayers have questioned the wisdom of taking their case to an Appeals Officer as they did not understand that the Appeals Officer has wider discretion to settle a case. Repeatedly, taxpayers ask me why they can not present testimony to a Revenue Agent or why the Revenue Agent will not negotiate a fixed dollar settlement agreement. It is because that is not their job. It is easy to see why many taxpayers become frustrated with the system. It is necessary to talk with the correct party in the correct division of the IRS. In such a large organization, that task alone can present an impossible problem.

Never, Never, Never Ignore an IRS Notice!!!

One of the most common mistakes made by a taxpayer is to ignore an IRS notice. The notice may take the form of a letter notifying you of interest or dividends that you failed to report. The IRS will request verification by mail that this income has been reported. If you ignore this notice, the IRS will assess additional taxes due. Once the IRS assesses taxes, they will send you collection notices. If you ignore these notices, the IRS will attempt to seize your bank accounts or levy your wages.

The IRS will not go away if you ignore its notices. The IRS can make assessments based on information it has. If you receive an audit notice, you should contact the Revenue Agent immediately. You can not hide or postpone the audit indefinitely.

Many of my clients receive notices to pay their taxes. They do not respond to these notices because they do not have the funds to satisfy the liability. This is the worst thing to do. You should respond to every letter or notice received from the IRS **in writing**. If you can not pay the liability, let the IRS know. Keep in touch!

Do Not Attend an Audit Unprepared . . . Or Else!

Most taxpayers go into the audit thinking that "the IRS can not prove I did anything wrong." If you approach the audit in this way, you will lose. The taxpayer always has the burden to prove that their tax return is accurate and complete as filed. Unlike our criminal justice system, where you are innocent until proven guilty, the IRS audit starts with the premise that the taxpayer must substantiate the positions taken on their tax return. You must prove that you are innocent. If you can not prove your income and deductions, the IRS will assess additional taxes.

Once I represented a taxpayer who handled the audit himself. He believed he had accurately filed his tax return. He did not compile his records. When the Revenue Agent asked for proof of his deductions, he wrote letters saying he was entitled to all of the deductions he had taken. He presented the Revenue Agent with a lot of information which was not organized. The Revenue Agent wrote a report disallowing all the claimed deductions over a period of years and proposed a deficiency of $400,000 in additional taxes, interest and penalties. Taxpayer had failed to prove he was entitled to the deductions on the tax return. Taxpayer retained me at this point. I reconstructed and compiled his records and requested an appellate conference. At that time I discovered that taxpayer was entitled to many deductions he had not taken. He also had taken some deductions that were erroneous. After one year of negotiating with the Appeals Officer, we agreed to pay a $15,000 deficiency. The taxpayer had one year of sleepless nights pending the outcome of the appeal, as he would have been wiped out financially if the original proposed assessment was valid. Throughout this entire process taxpayer kept telling me "he had done nothing wrong." This was not important. The important issue was to provide **proof**.

In another case, I represented a taxpayer who the IRS claimed had failed to report all his income. The taxpayer could not verify where the money came from for all the deposits into his bank account. When I tried to reconstruct his cash savings from prior years, I could not. The taxpayer would not provide proof because he kept insisting that he did nothing wrong. His statements were not adequate proof to win the case.

Schedule the Audit Conference so That You Will Have Adequate Time to Compile Your Records. Do Not Be Intimidated into Submitting Information Which is Incomplete.

Taxpayers erroneously believe that the Revenue Agent will be lenient if they comply with the Revenue Agent's time schedule. This is not true. It is better to be late and accurate, than file erroneous information. Remember that the Revenue Agent's job is to assess taxes and raise revenue to ensure compliance with the tax laws of our country. The fact that you comply with the Revenue Agent's time schedule will not alter this fact.

If the IRS notifies you of an audit, you should work with the Revenue Agent to establish a convenient time to meet. Usually the IRS will try to schedule a meeting in the initial audit notice. This time may or may not be convenient for you. This time may or may not give you adequate time to prepare for the audit. The IRS has recently issued final regulations which state that the goal of the IRS is to "maximize convenience to the taxpayer within the constraints of sound and efficient tax administration in setting the time and place of the examination."

Under the provisions of the Internal Revenue Code, the examination shall take place at a time that is "reasonable under the circumstances." This provision requires that the taxpayer have a right to some extent to dictate the time and place of the audit. In my practice, I nearly always require additional time to prepare for the audit. You have the right to request an extension of time.

Many times I have had Revenue Agent threaten or imply enforcement action or preparation of an adverse report if certain information was not submitted by a certain date. In many instances, it is just not possible to comply with their time table as it might take a long period of time to request certain information. Be firm in requesting an extension and do not be intimidated. Keep the Revenue Agent informed about when the information will be available.

Normally I will write a letter to the Revenue Agent requesting that the date be postponed either because the taxpayer's schedule is such that taxpayer can not compile the information in a timely manner or the information to substantiate something is not currently available and must be requested (such as lost or incomplete records). I will keep the Revenue Agent informed about when the information will be forwarded and when we can meet. In some instances it has taken the taxpayer over 6 months to prepare for the audit. Do not be intimidated into appearing at the audit earlier than necessary without the appropriate records. The Revenue Agent will not be lenient with you because you met his time schedule.

Compile and Organize Your Records Before the Audit. The First Step in Winning the Attack by the IRS is to Present Proof of Your Income and Deductions in a Way That Will Satisfy the Revenue Agent.

Many taxpayers have asked me what to bring to an audit or how to prove their deductions. The Revenue Agent will tell the taxpayer that "proof" for a certain deduction is not sufficient. The Revenue Agent's determination of whether or not you have submitted sufficient evidence is not conclusive. Taxpayers always have appeal rights. Proof in court can take the form of canceled checks, logs, receipts, bank statements or testimony. Do not be intimidated into concession if the Revenue Agent claims that your proof is not sufficient. It may be sufficient upon appeal. Usually the Revenue Agent will not accept taxpayer testimony as verification, but upon appeal the IRS will consider this evidence. Remember, the Revenue Agent's report is not binding.

Usually upon receipt of a notice for audit, the IRS includes a list of items that it would like to verify. After the initial audit meeting, it is likely that you will receive a document production or information request that lists additional information needed. Normally, I will compile what I call my "black book". This book indexes each document request. I make copies of the relevant data to support each request and include it in the black book. If information is not available or the request is unreasonable, I so state. I include taxpayer statements or narratives where appropriate. I also include schedules, amendments to the tax returns (if errors are found) or other relevant information. I then make a copy of all the items I have submitted so I can have a record of all the documents examined in the audit. This is especially useful in large cases. In a recent case, there were 10 document requests and accordingly, I had compiled 10 black books, all indexed for submission.

The important thing about the black book is that the Revenue Agent knows I am prepared to appeal the case if necessary and I will not have to undergo additional factual development or legal analysis. I have done all my homework in advance. The Revenue Agent also is aware of the fact that on appeal, additional evidence and the hazards of litigation will be considered in reaching a settlement. The taxpayer's case is complete and ready to go to appeals.

Recently, I had a case where the IRS was challenging a deduction by a corporation for reasonable salaries to an officer. The assessment by the auditor was for over $1 million dollars. I came into the case at that point and asked for an examination reconsideration. A new Revenue Agent became involved in the case. Before the meeting I drafted a complete legal memorandum to support our position on the reasonableness of the compensation. The legal memorandum analyzed the relevant case law as it applied in our situation. I drafted the legal memorandum as if I were appearing in court that day. I also attached factual affidavits, average salary surveys, newspaper articles about the taxpayer and the business and other evidence to support our position. I outlined the proposed testimony if the case was to go to court. At the meeting, I informed the Revenue Agent of my prior background in tax litigation. After consideration of our submission, the Revenue Agent offered to settle for $250,000. I declined as I informed the Revenue Agent that I believed the facts presented would sustain my client's position in court. He then offered us a $60,000 settlement. I informed him that a trial would cost taxpayer $25,000 and we were prepared to fight. The Revenue Agent's final offer was for $22,000. We accepted. Taxpayer was happy to avoid the uncertainty of a 3 year IRS battle. I believe that the IRS offered the settlement because the Revenue Agent knew that taxpayer was ready to do battle and I was well-prepared on his behalf.

Many taxpayers tell me that they have time to prepare if they do not prevail at the audit level. The biggest mistake in any case is not being fully prepared at the beginning. If you wait until your case is docketed in court, you have already lost half the battle.

SURVIVAL #6 STRATEGY

Be Careful if the Revenue Agent Asks You to File Form 4822—Statement of Annual Estimated Personal and Family Living Expenses. The Agent is Trying to Determine if You Have Unreported Income. Use Income and Expenses for the Year in Issue, Not the Current Year.

Many times the Revenue Agent will request Form 4822 (see page 16) from the taxpayer. Usually the Revenue Agent makes this request when he or she believes that you have unreported income. The taxpayer has the burden to show that the income reported on his tax return is correct.

In conjunction with Form 4822, the taxpayer will also be requested to reconstruct his cash on hand at the beginning of the year and at the end of the year. Usually the IRS asks for this information for a period of 2 or 3 previous years and you must reconstruct expenditures and receipts. This is only one method to verify income. If the taxpayer has his own business and relies on cash income and cash payments of expenses, it may be the only method of verification available. However, if a taxpayer is an employee and maintains bank accounts, it will be more expeditious for taxpayer to persuade the Revenue Agent to accept income verification based on W-2's and bank statements.

The Form 4822 will imply that you have unreported income in those cases where the yearly estimated expenses exceed the income you reported. You should be careful to fill out Form 4822 using the actual expenses for the year in issue, not current expenses.

The IRS uses three methods to verify your income reported on your tax return. The IRS considers any unexplained money or increases in property that exceed reported income and cash resources unreported income. If your assets net of liabilities increase substantially from one year to the next year, the IRS will require you to verify that reported income net of expenses accounts for the increase to net worth. If it does not, you must prove that the increase in net worth was due to gifts, inheritance or other investments that are not taxable.

The starting point in this analysis is normally your assets minus your liabilities at the beginning of the year. The IRS examines bank records, prior income tax returns, real estate records, and your books and records to determine your actual net worth. Increases in your net worth relate either to (i) prior cash or income accumulated, (ii) current income, or (iii) nontaxable gifts or inheritances. You must corroborate that the net increase is not due to unreported taxable income. Otherwise the IRS will take the position that you have unreported income that is subject to tax.

The second method for verifying your income is the expenditure method. Under this method, the IRS will examine your expenses for the year. If your expenses exceed your reported income, the IRS will claim that you had more income than reported and such income is from taxable sources. The starting point for this inquiry is the Form 4822.

The last method used by the IRS to verify income is the bank deposits method. The IRS will examine your bank statements to determine the source of all cash and non-cash deposits. The Revenue Agent will total all your deposits and then subtract out loans, deposits from other accounts, bank transfers, gifts, inheritances, reimbursements or other non-taxable items to arrive at your taxable income.

The Revenue Agent normally uses these methods when you

have a cash business or when the taxpayer has inconsistent records. That is why it is very important for you to go into the audit
with consistent and organized books and records. If you do have
a cash business it is important to keep daily logs, make periodic
bank deposits and keep complete books and records using an established accounting system.

Form **4822** (Rev. 6-83)		Department of the Treasury - Internal Revenue Service STATEMENT OF ANNUAL ESTIMATED PERSONAL AND FAMILY EXPENSES			

TAXPAYER'S NAME AND ADDRESS

Mr. and Mrs TAX PAYER
123 TAX BlVD
WAshington DC

TAX YEAR ENDED

	ITEM	BY CASH	BY CHECK	TOTAL	REMARKS
1. PERSONAL EXPENSES	Groceries and outside meals	2400	500	2900	
	Clothing	1000		1000	
	Laundry and dry cleaning		600	600	
	Barber, beauty shop, and cosmetics	240		240	
	Education *(tuition, room, board, books, etc.)*				
	Recreation, entertainment, vacations				
	Dues *(clubs, lodge, etc.)*		100	100	
	Gifts and allowances		250	250	
	Life and accident insurance		5000	5000	
	Federal taxes *(income, FICA, etc.)*		10,000	10,000	
2. HOUSEHOLD EXPENSES	Rent				
	Mortgage payments *(including interest)*		12,000	12,000	
	Utilities *(electricity, gas, telephone, water, etc.)*		2400	2400	
	Domestic help				
	Home insurance		1000	1000	
	Repairs and improvements		2000	2000	
	Child care				
	·				
3. AUTO EXPENSES	Gasoline, oil, grease, wash				
	Tires, batteries, repairs, tags				
	Insurance		2400	2400	
	Auto payments *(including interest)*				
	Lease of auto		6000	6000	
4. DEDUCTIBLE ITEMS	Contributions				
	Medical Expenses — Insurance		3600	3600	
	Drugs		500	500	
	Doctors, hospitals, etc.		700	700	
	Taxes — Real estate *(not included in 2. above)*				
	Personal property				
	Income *(State and local)*		1500	1500	
	Interest *(not included in 2. and 3. above)*				
	Miscellaneous — Alimony				
	Union dues				
5. PERSONAL ASSETS, ETC.	Stocks and bonds				
	Furniture, appliances, jewelry				
	Loans to others				
	Boat				
	TOTALS ▶	3640	48550	52,190	

* U S GOVERNMENT PRINTING OFFICE 1983-381-541/5272

Form 4822 (Rev. 6-83)

12/18/91 page 746,521

SURVIVAL #1 STRATEGY

Take Advantage of Any Additional Deductions to Which You Are Entitled and Correct Any Mistakes You Made on Your Tax Return as Originally Filed.

In many instances, you may discover in preparing for the audit, that you have failed to take advantage of additional deductions. You may need to file amended tax returns. About 21% of all audits result no additional assessments or a refund! Sometimes, the Revenue Agent may refuse to consider additional deductions or reductions in income. This is contrary to the IRS's regulations. These regulations provide that during an audit "the taxpayer has the right to point out to the examining officer any amounts included in the return that are not taxable, or any deductions that the taxpayer failed to claim on the tax return." The taxpayer has the right under the IRS regulations to reduce the income reported on the tax return if such amounts were not income or the right to assert any additional deductions not previously taken.

In one case, I discovered that taxpayer had over reported his income by $163,000! He had loaned the money previously to the company. The company had repaid him 3 years later. The accountant who had prepared the return had treated this amount as salary. He had paid income and employment taxes on this sum. We immediately notified the Revenue Agent who claimed that there was no proof as to this loan repayment. Later, the taxpayer's testimony sufficed and ultimately a refund was due and owing.

In my experience, many times taxpayers are due refunds. These requests for refunds should be filed on Form 1040X or Form 843 (see pages 19–21). Many taxpayers fail to take advantage of legitimate deductions because the tax laws are complex and it is difficult for the typical taxpayer to know all the potential entitlements to deductions. Even when taxpayers do consult an accountant, they should be aware that in many instances the accountant's role is to accurately compile data and not to do any financial or tax planning. In that situation, the accountant's job is to accurately compile the information supplied by you. If you call a distribution "salary," the accountant is likely to stop any inquiry at this point. This salary will be included in your income even though it may be a repayment of a loan, a dividend not subject to employment tax or non-taxable return of your capital.

Form 1040X
(Rev. November 1991)

Department of the Treasury—Internal Revenue Service

Amended U.S. Individual Income Tax Return

▶ See separate instructions.

OMB No. 1545-0091
Expires 10-31-94

This return is for calendar year ▶ 19 ___ , OR fiscal year ended ▶ ___ , 19 **92** .

Your first name and initial **A**	Last name **TAXPAYer**	Your social security number **000 11 2222**
If a joint return, spouse's first name and initial	Last name	Spouse's social security number
Home address (number and street). (If you have a P.O. box, see instructions.) **123 TAX BLVD**	Apt. no.	Telephone number (optional) ( )
City, town or post office, state, and ZIP code. (If you have a foreign address, see instructions.) **Washington DC**		For Paperwork Reduction Act Notice, see page 1 of separate instructions.

Please print or type

Enter name and address as shown on original return (if same as above, write "Same"). If changing from separate to joint return, enter names and addresses from original return.

SAME

A Service center where original return was filed
Philadelphia, PA.

B Has original return been changed or audited by the IRS? ☐ Yes ☒ No
If "No," have you been notified that it will be? . . . . ☐ Yes ☒ No
If "Yes," identify the IRS office ▶

C Are you amending your return to include any item (loss, credit, deduction, other tax benefit, or income) relating to a tax shelter required to be registered? . . . . ☐ Yes ☒ No
If "Yes," you **MUST** attach Form 8271, Investor Reporting of Tax Shelter Registration Number.

D Filing status claimed. (**Note:** *You cannot change from joint to separate returns after the due date has passed.*)
On original return ▶ ☒ Single ☐ Married filing joint return ☐ Married filing separate return ☐ Head of household ☐ Qualifying widow(er)
On this return ▶ ☒ Single ☐ Married filing joint return ☐ Married filing separate return ☐ Head of household ☐ Qualifying widow(er)

Income and Deductions (see instructions) (**Note:** *Be sure to complete page 2.*)		A. As originally reported or as adjusted (see instructions)	B. Net change—Increase or (Decrease)—explain on page 2	C. Correct amount
1 Total income	1	10,000	0	10,000
2 Adjustments to income	2	0	0	0
3 Adjusted gross income (subtract line 2 from line 1)	3	10,000	0	10,000
4 Itemized deductions or standard deduction . .	4	5,000	6000	11,000
5 Subtract line 4 from line 3	5	5,000		0
6 Exemptions (if changing, fill in Parts I and II on page 2) .	6	2,000		0
7 Taxable income (subtract line 6 from line 5)	7	3,000		0
8 Tax (see instructions). (Method used in col. C.................)	8	1,000		0
9 Credits (see instructions)	9	0		0
10 Subtract line 9 from line 8. Enter the result but not less than zero .	10	1,000		0
11 Other taxes (such as self-employment tax, alternative minimum tax) .	11	0		0
12 Total tax (add lines 10 and 11)	12	1,000		0
13 Federal income tax withheld and excess social security, Medicare, and RRTA taxes withheld	13			
14 Estimated tax payments	14			
15 Earned income credit	15			
16 Credits for Federal tax on fuels, regulated investment company, etc.	16			
17 Amount paid with Form 4868, Form 2688, or Form 2350 (application for extension of time to file) . . .			17	
18 Amount paid with original return plus additional tax paid after it was filed			18	1,000
19 Add lines 13 through 18 in column C			19	1,000

Tax Liability

Payments

Refund or Amount You Owe

20 Overpayment, if any, as shown on original return (or as previously adjusted by the IRS) . . .		20	0
21 Subtract line 20 from line 19 (see instructions)		21	1,000
22 **AMOUNT YOU OWE.** If line 12, col. C, is more than line 21, enter the difference and see instructions . .		22	
23 **REFUND** to be received. If line 12, column C, is less than line 21, enter the difference . . .		23	1,000

Please Sign Here

Under penalties of perjury, I declare that I have filed an original return and that I have examined this amended return, including accompanying schedules and statements, and to the best of my knowledge and belief, this amended return is true, correct, and complete. Declaration of preparer (other than taxpayer) is based on all information of which the preparer has any knowledge.

▶ **A. Taxpayer** | **10-15-93** ▶
Your signature | Date | Spouse's signature (if joint return, BOTH must sign) | Date

Paid Preparer's Use Only

Preparer's signature ▶		Date	Check if self-employed ☐	Preparer's social security no.
Firm's name (or yours if self-employed) and address ▶			E.I. No.	
			ZIP code	

Cat. No. 11360L

Form 1040X (Rev. 11-91)   Page **2**

Part I — Exemptions (see Form 1040 or Form 1040A instructions)

If you are not changing your exemptions, do not complete this part.
If claiming more exemptions, complete lines 24–30 and, if applicable, line 31.
If claiming fewer exemptions, complete lines 24–29.

		A. Number originally reported	B. Net change	C. Correct number
24	Yourself and spouse			
	Caution: If your parents (or someone else) can claim you as a dependent (even if they chose not to), you cannot claim an exemption for yourself.			
25	Your dependent children who lived with you			
26	Your dependent children who did not live with you due to divorce or separation			
27	Other dependents			
28	Total number of exemptions (add lines 24 through 27)			
29	For tax year 1991, if the amount on page 1, line 3, is more than $75,000, see the instructions. If line 3 is $75,000 or less, multiply $2,150 by the number of exemptions claimed on line 28. For tax year 1990, use $2,050; for tax year 1989, use $2,000; for tax year 1988, use $1,950. Enter the result here and on page 1, line 6.			

30 Dependents (children and other) not claimed on original return:

No. of your children on line 30 who lived with you ▶ ☐

(a) Dependent's name (first, initial, and last name)	(b) Check if under age 1 (under age 2 if a 1989 or 1990 return; under age 5 if a 1988 return)	(c) If age 1 or older (age 2 or older if a 1989 or 1990 return; age 5 or older if a 1988 return), enter dependent's social security number	(d) Dependent's relationship to you	(e) No. of months lived in your home	
		: :			No. of your children on line 30 who didn't live with you due to divorce or separation (see instructions) ▶ ☐
		: :			
		: :			No. of other dependents listed on line 30 ▶ ☐
	·	: :			

31 If your child listed on line 30 didn't live with you but is claimed as your dependent under a pre-1985 agreement, check here . . . . ▶ ☐

Part II — Explanation of Changes to Income, Deductions, and Credits

Enter the line number from page 1 for each item you are changing and give the reason for each change. Attach all supporting forms and schedules for items changed. Be sure to include your name and social security number on any attachments.

If the change pertains to a net operating loss carryback or a general business credit carryback, attach the schedule or form that shows the year in which the loss or credit occurred. See instructions. Also, check here . . . . ▶ ☐

line 4: To take into account itemized deductions not previously recorded for mortgage interest (see attached Form 1099)

Part III — Presidential Election Campaign Fund

Checking below will not increase your tax or reduce your refund.

If you did not previously want to have $1 go to the fund but now want to, check here . . . . ▶ ☐
If a joint return and your spouse did not previously want to have $1 go to the fund but now wants to, check here . . . . . ▶ ☐

Form **843** (Rev. December 1987) Department of the Treasury Internal Revenue Service	**Claim** ▶ See Instructions on back.	OMB No. 1545-0024 Expires 9/30/90

If your claim is for an overpayment of income taxes, do NOT use this form. (See Instructions.)
(Use this form ONLY if your claim involves one of the taxes shown on line 8 or a refund or abatement of interest or penalties.)

Please type or print	Name of taxpayer or purchaser of stamps TAX, INC.	Telephone number (optional) ( )
	Number and street 100 TAX BLVD.	
	City, town, or post office, state, and ZIP code Washington DC	

Fill in applicable items—Use attachments if necessary

1 Your social security number	2 Spouse's social security number	3 Employer identification number 11-00044

4 Name and address shown on return if different from above

Same

5 Period—prepare separate form for each tax period From **3rd Qtr.** , 19**91** , to , 19	6 Amount to be refunded or abated $ 1,000

7 Dates of payment   8-1-91

8 Type of tax or penalty
☒ Employment ☐ Estate ☐ Excise ☐ Gift ☐ Stamp ☐ Penalty IRC section ▶

9 Kind of return filed
☐ 706 ☐ 709 ☐ 720 IRS No. (s) ▶ . ☐ 940 ☒ 941 ☐ 990-PF ☐ 2290 ☐ 4720
☐ Other (specify) ▶

10 If this claim involves refund of excise taxes on gasoline or special fuels, please indicate your tax year for income tax purposes.

11 Explain why you believe this claim should be allowed and show computation of tax refund or abatement of interest or penalty.

This is a claim for erroneously paid employment taxes

Under penalties of perjury, I declare that I have examined this claim, including accompanying schedules and statements, and to the best of my knowledge and belief it is true, correct, and complete.

A. Taxpayer, President
Signature (Title, if applicable)   Date

Signature   Date | Director's Stamp
(Date received) |

For Internal Revenue Service Use Only
☐ Refund of taxes illegally, erroneously, or excessively collected
☐ Refund of amount paid for stamps unused, or used in error or excess
☐ Abatement of tax assessed (not applicable to estate or gift taxes)

For Paperwork Reduction Act Notice, see Instructions on back.   Form **843** (Rev. 12-87)

SURVIVAL #8 STRATEGY

Know the Techniques of the Revenue Agent. Go to the Audit Knowing What You Are Going to be Asked so You Can Prepare in Advance.

The audit of all tax returns is covered by a manual called "Examination Technique Guidelines". There are also parts of the Internal Revenue Manual that deal with audit procedures. The IRS provides procedures for general audits, as well as by industry. If you are familiar with the general questions asked on an audit and also specific issues that may come up because of the industry you are in, you can anticipate what questions will be asked and you can prepare.

The purpose of any examination is to verify records. This is the reason for the audit. The Revenue Agent has a series of audit checklists that need to complied with. Failure to keep adequate records is the #1 reason for disallowance of a deduction. Remember that the Revenue Agent's job is to identify items for adjustment, verify items on your tax return, and ascertain whether the positions taken on your tax return are in compliance with the Internal Revenue Code. Substantiation and verification are the purpose of the audit meeting.

Taxpayer's are required by law to maintain and keep books and records of account sufficient to establish the items of income, deduction or credit reported on the tax return. These records may consist of:

◊ Primary records such as invoices, vouchers, bills, receipts, and canceled checks; and

◊ Secondary records such as your permanent books and
   records.

If you do not maintain adequate books and records, the IRS
may issue a Notice of Inadequate Books and Records. If you receive this notice you will be subject to audit for the following three
years so that the IRS can ascertain whether you are complying
with the Internal Revenue Code requirements. This can be costly
in terms of your time and your expense.

Many times taxpayers will ask me why the Revenue Agent
keeps asking for certain information. They feel that they are being harassed. They will ask me whether the requests are normal
or excessive. Usually, the Revenue Agent is following audit guidelines. The Revenue Agent is asking the taxpayer for the same information that all other taxpayers are asked on similar issues.

The Seven Secrets to Handling a Tax Audit.

There are seven simple steps to handling a tax audit:

◊ Assemble and organize your records. Make copies for the Revenue Agent. Use a black book to index your records.

◊ Remove all material which is not relevant from your records. Keep the focus of the audit on the books and records that are relevant to your tax return. Never give the Revenue Agent a box of all your canceled checks and receipts for the entire year.

◊ Do not volunteer information. Respond solely to the question the Revenue Agent is asking you.

◊ If you are going to use an attorney or accountant, bring them in at the beginning of the audit so there is consistency in the audit and your representative can protect your rights from the start.

◊ Ask the Revenue Agent to make a written request for all document production so that you have a record of what he or she has requested and what you have provided.

◊ Be available for questions. If you can resolve an issue early in the audit, you can focus on the more important issues.

◊ If the Revenue Agent indicates that some adjustments are in order, ask for a list of proposed adjustments and then try to narrow the list before the Revenue Agent issues the final report. This will also help to narrow the issues that are problems.

Remember that **proof** is the key to winning!! Your job is to produce enough information to convince the Revenue Agent that an adjustment is not appropriate.

When Should You Consult Counsel? The Earlier You Obtain Legal Advice, the More Money You Will Save in the Long Run.

The cases that are the most difficult and expensive to win are those cases where I am called in after the audit. In those situations, I have to start the audit from the beginning. The Revenue Agent normally has a large amount of inconsistent evidence by this time and I have an uphill battle. In many cases, the taxpayer has disclosed information that is confusing the issues or has provided inadequate proof. I have to establish the evidence and negate prior erroneous information submitted by the taxpayer.

Many times taxpayers have told me that they were handling the audit by themselves because the agent was "being nice and helping them get through it" so everything was under control. The only problem is that it is not the Revenue Agent's job to help you win.

You should obtain legal advice in the following situations:

◊ You are involved in a lengthy audit with many legal and factual issues.

◊ You are involved in a civil or criminal fraud investigation.

◊ Your case involves a potentially large deficiency.

◊ Your case involves an unclear and complex legal issue.

◊ You do not know how to prove your case. You have inadequate books and records.

◊ You owe the IRS money that you can not afford to pay and you have not filed your tax returns for a number of years.

◊ You want to WIN. You feel strongly about your position and you know the IRS will litigate the issue.

If you wish to have an accountant, lawyer or enrolled agent represent you, the first step is to file a Power of Attorney (see page 28) with each office of the IRS which has control over your case.

Generally, once you execute the Power of Attorney, your representative will have the power to discuss your confidential tax information, review and request your statement of account, and execute extensions of the statute of limitations and closing agreements on your behalf.

Your representative must have a power of attorney from you to request information or negotiate on your behalf. The IRS can not legally disclose your confidential tax information to third parties. IRS employees are personally liable for unauthorized disclosure of your tax information.

The most important thing to remember in filling out the Power of Attorney is to include all taxes (income and employment) and all periods that your representative might need to discuss. This can include periods outside the audited years.

After filing the Power of Attorney, the IRS will send all notices to your representative. The IRS should be dealing solely with that designated party and to protect your interests and your rights you should refer any IRS employee who contacts you to your representative.

Form **2848**	**Power of Attorney**	OMB No. 1545-0150
(Rev. March 1991)	**and Declaration of Representative**	Expires 5-31-93
Department of the Treasury Internal Revenue Service	▶ For Paperwork Reduction and Privacy Act Notice, see the Instructions.	

Part I   Power of Attorney

1   Taxpayer Information

Taxpayer name(s) and address (Please type or print.)	Social security number(s)	Employer identification number
A. TAXpayer 123 TAX Blvd. Washington D.c.	000 : 00 : 0000	
	Daytime telephone number ( )	Plan number (if applicable)

hereby appoint(s) the following representative(s) as attorney(s)-in-fact:

2   Representative(s) (Please type or print.)

Name and address	
XYZ, Esquire 1700 K St NW Washington DC.	CAF No. .... Telephone No. (202) 222-2222 Fax No. ( ).......................... Check if new: Address . . . ☐ Telephone No. ☐
Name and address	CAF No. .... Telephone No. ( )......................... Fax No. ( )......................... Check if new: Address . . . ☐ Telephone No. ☐
Name and address	CAF No. .... Telephone No. ( )......................... Fax No. ( )......................... Check if new: Address . . . ☐ Telephone No. ☐

to represent the taxpayer(s) before the Internal Revenue Service for the following tax matters:

3   Tax Matters

Type of Tax (Income, Employment, Excise, etc.)	Tax Form Number (1040, 941, 720, etc.)	Year(s) or Period(s)
Income	1040	1988-1991

4   Specific Use Not Recorded on Centralized Authorization File (CAF).—If the power of attorney is for a specific use not recorded on CAF, please check this box. (See the instructions for *Specific Use Not Recorded on CAF* on page 4.)   . . . . ▶ ☐

5   Acts Authorized.—The representatives are authorized to receive and inspect confidential tax information and to perform any and all acts that I can perform with respect to the tax matters described in line 3, for example, the authority to sign any agreements, consents, or other documents. The authority does not include the power to receive refund checks or the power to sign certain returns. (See instructions.)
List any specific additions or deletions to the acts otherwise authorized in this power of attorney: ....
....
....

Note: *In general, an unenrolled preparer of tax returns cannot sign any document for a taxpayer. See Revenue Procedure 81-38, printed as Pub. 470, for more information.*

Note: *The tax matters partner/person of a partnership or S corporation is not permitted to authorize representatives to perform certain acts. See the instructions for more information.*

6   Receipt of Refund Checks.—If you want to authorize a representative named in line 2 to receive, **BUT NOT TO ENDORSE OR CASH,** refund checks, initial here _____ and list the name of that representative below. ▼

Name of representative to receive refund check(s) ▶

Cat. No. 11980J

Form **2848** (Rev. 3-91)

Form 2848 (Rev. 3 91)   Page **2**

7 Notices and Communications.—Notices and other written communications will be sent to the first representative listed in line 2.

   a If you want the second representative listed to receive such notices and communications, check this box . . . . ▶ ☐

   b If you do not want any notices or communications sent to your representative, check this box . . . . ▶ ☐

8 Retention/Revocation of Prior Power(s) of Attorney.—The filing of this power of attorney automatically revokes all earlier power(s) of attorney on file with the Internal Revenue Service for the **same** tax matters and years or periods covered by this document. If you do not want to revoke a prior power of attorney, check here . . . . ▶ ☐

   YOU MUST ATTACH A COPY OF ANY POWER OF ATTORNEY YOU WANT TO REMAIN IN EFFECT.

9 Signature of Taxpayer(s).—If a tax matter concerns a joint return, **both** husband and wife must sign if joint representation is requested, otherwise, see the instructions. If signed by a corporate officer, partner, guardian, tax matters partner/person, executor, receiver, administrator, or trustee on behalf of the taxpayer, I certify that I have the authority to execute this form on behalf of the taxpayer.

   ▶ **If this power of attorney is not signed, it will be returned.**

A. Taxpayer	11-15-93	
Signature	Date	Title (if applicable)

Print Name		

Signature	Date	Title (if applicable)

Print Name		

Part II Declaration of Representative

Under penalties of perjury, I declare that:

   ● I am not currently under suspension or disbarment from practice before the Internal Revenue Service;

   ● I am aware of regulations contained in Treasury Department Circular No. 230 (31 CFR, Part 10), as amended, concerning the practice of attorneys, certified public accountants, enrolled agents, enrolled actuaries, and others;

   ● I am authorized to represent the taxpayer(s) identified in Part I for the tax matter(s) specified there; and

   ● I am one of the following:

     a Attorney—a member in good standing of the bar of the highest court of the jurisdiction shown below.

     b Certified Public Accountant—duly qualified to practice as a certified public accountant in the jurisdiction shown below.

     c Enrolled Agent—enrolled as an agent under the requirements of Treasury Department Circular No. 230.

     d Officer—a bona fide officer of the taxpayer organization.

     e Full-Time Employee—a full-time employee of the taxpayer.

     f Family Member—a member of the taxpayer's immediate family (*i.e.*, spouse, parent, child, brother, or sister).

     g Enrolled Actuary—enrolled as an actuary by the Joint Board for the Enrollment of Actuaries under 29 U.S.C. 1242 (the authority to practice before the Service is limited by section 10.3(d)(1) of Treasury Department Circular No. 230).

     h Unenrolled Return Preparer—an unenrolled return preparer under section 10.7(a)(7) of Treasury Department Circular No. 230.

▶ **If this power of attorney is not signed, it will be returned.**

Designation —Insert above letter (a–h)	Jurisdiction (state) or Enrollment Card No.	Signature	Date
a	DC	X4z	11-15-93

SURVIVAL #**11** STRATEGY

Know What Forms You Are Executing During an Audit. Know What Rights You Are Giving Up and Know What Your Options Are if You Do Not Execute the Forms Requested by the Revenue Agent.

The most common form that the IRS asks taxpayers to execute during the audit is the Form 872 or Form 872-A (see page 32). The Revenue Agent will request these forms from you if the statute of limitations on assessment of additional taxes is about to expire. You must execute this form before the statute of limitations expires. If you do not, there can be no assessment.

The Revenue Agent has several alternatives if the statute of limitations is about to expire. Normally he will request that you execute Form 872-A. That is an open ended consent. The period for assessment remains open until the Revenue Agent completes the audit. On the other hand, Form 872 sets a specific date for expiration of the period to make an assessment.

If you do not execute this consent the Revenue Agent will issue a Statutory Notice of Deficiency which suspends the statute of limitations, but leaves you with many issues set up by the Revenue Agent. The IRS also has the power to make jeopardy assessments or accelerate the audit, thereby depriving you of the time necessary to submit all your evidence. On the other hand, the Revenue Agent could close the examination.

My usual advice is to sign the consent. This gives you and the Revenue Agent a chance to narrow the issues and present your case to the fullest extent. You can sign a limited consent as to a few specific issues. Signing the consent also allows you to exhaust all of your administration appeals before heading to Tax Court.

The IRS may also request that you sign a Form 870 at the end of the audit wherein you agree to the immediate assessment of tax.

When the IRS asks you to sign this Form you have the following options:

◊ You can agree with the report and sign (see page 36) which permits immediate assessment of the proposed deficiency.

◊ You can disagree and request consideration of your case by the regional appeals office. If the amount in controversy is over $2500 you will need to file a written protest within 30 days and request an appellate conference.

◊ You can do nothing. You will receive a Statutory Notice of Deficiency that will allow you to file a petition with the Tax Court. If you decide not to file in the Tax Court, the IRS will forward a bill to you. You can pay the bill and then file a claim for refund in the appropriate Federal District Court or the Claims Court.

Form **872-A** (Rev. October 1987)	Department of the Treasury — Internal Revenue Service **Special Consent to Extend the Time to Assess Tax**	In reply refer to: SSN or EIN

<u>   A . TAXpayer   </u>
                               (Name(s))

taxpayer(s) of <u> 123 TAX BlVD. Washington DC   </u>
                   (Number, Street, City or Town, State, ZIP Code)
and the District Director of Internal Revenue or Regional Director of Appeals consent and agree as follows:

(1) The amount(s) of any Federal <u> income   </u> tax due on any return(s) made by or
                                      (Kind of tax)
for the above taxpayer(s) for the period(s) ended <u> 1990   </u>
may be assessed on or before the 90th (ninetieth) day after: (a) the Internal Revenue Service office considering the case receives Form 872-T, Notice of Termination of Special Consent to Extend the Time to Assess Tax, from the taxpayer(s); or (b) the Internal Revenue Service mails Form 872-T to the taxpayer(s); or (c) the Internal Revenue Service mails a notice of deficiency for such period(s); except that if a notice of deficiency is sent to the taxpayer(s), the time for assessing the tax for the period(s) stated in the notice of deficiency will end 60 days after the period during which the making of an assessment is prohibited. A final adverse determination subject to declaratory judgment under sections 7428, 7476, or 7477 of the Internal Revenue Code will not terminate this agreement.

(2) This agreement ends on the earlier of the above expiration date or the assessment date of an increase in the above tax or the overassessment date of a decrease in the above tax that reflects the final determination of tax and the final administrative appeals consideration. An assessment or overassessment for one period covered by this agreement will t end this agreement for any other period it covers. Some assessments do not reflect a final determination and appeals consideration and therefore will not terminate the agreement before the expiration date. Examples are assessments of: (a) tax under a partial agreement; (b) tax in jeopardy; (c) tax to correct mathematical or clerical errors; (d) tax reported on amended returns; and (e) advance payments. In addition, unassessed payments, such as amounts treated by the Service as cash bonds and advance payments not assessed by the Service, will not terminate this agreement before the expiration date determined in (1) above. This agreement ends on the date determined in (1) above regardless of any assessment for any period includible in a report to the Joint Committee on Taxation submitted under section 6405 of the Internal Revenue Code.

(3) This agreement will not reduce the period of time otherwise provided by law for making such assessment.

(4) The taxpayer(s) may file a claim for credit or refund and the Service may credit or refund the tax within 6 (six) months after this agreement ends.

(Signature instructions and space for signature are on the back of this form)   Form **872-A** (Rev. 10-87)

MAKING THIS CONSENT WILL NOT DEPRIVE THE TAXPAYER(S) OF ANY APPEAL RIGHTS TO WHICH THEY WOULD OTHERWISE BE ENTITLED.

YOUR SIGNATURE HERE ➤ _A. Taxpayer_ _____   _____
                                                                  (Date signed)

SPOUSE'S SIGNATURE ➤ _____   _____
                                                                  (Date signed)

TAXPAYER'S REPRESENTATIVE
SIGN HERE ➤ _____   _____
                                                                  (Date signed)

CORPORATE
NAME ➤ _____

CORPORATE   _____   _____
OFFICER(S)   *(Title)*   *(Date signed)*
SIGN HERE   _____   _____
                                (Title)   *(Date signed)*

_____   _____
DISTRICT DIRECTOR OF INTERNAL REVENUE   REGIONAL DIRECTOR OF APPEALS

BY _____   _____
                (Signature and Title)   *(Date signed)*

Instructions

If this consent is for income tax, self-employment tax, or FICA tax on tips and is made for any year(s) for which a joint return was filed, both husband and wife must sign the original and copy of this form unless one, acting under a power of attorney, signs as agent for the other. The signatures must match the names as they appear on the front of this form.

If this consent is for gift tax and the donor and the donor's spouse elected to have gifts to third persons considered as made one-half by each, both husband and wife must sign the original and copy of this form unless one, acting under a power of attorney, signs as agent for the other. The signatures must match the names as they appear on the front of this form.

If this consent is for Chapter 41, 42, or 43 taxes involving a partnership, only one authorized partner need sign.

If you are an attorney or agent of the taxpayer(s), you may sign this consent provided the action is specifically authorized by a power of attorney. If the power of attorney was not previously filed, you must include it with this form.

If you are acting as a fiduciary *(such as executor, administrator, trustee, etc.)* and you sign this consent, attach Form 56, Notice Concerning Fiduciary Relationship, unless it was previously filed.

If the taxpayer is a corporation, sign this consent with the corporate name followed by the signature and title of the officer(s) authorized to sign.

If this consent is for Chapter 42 taxes, a separate Form 872-A should be completed for each potential disqualified person or entity that may have been involved in a taxable transaction during the related tax year. See Revenue Ruling 75-391, 1975-2 C.B. 446.

Form **872-A** (Rev. 10-87)

Form 872. Consent of Fixing Period of Limitation Upon Assessment of Income Tax.

Form **872** (Rev. August 1988)	Department of the Treasury—Internal Revenue Service **Consent to Extend the Time to Assess Tax**	In Reply Refer To:
		SSN or EIN

_____ *A. TAXPAYER* _____
                                      (Name(s))

taxpayer(s) of ..._123 TAX BLVD., washington D.C._____
                                      (Number, Street, City or Town, State, ZIP Code)

and the District Director of Internal Revenue or Regional Director of Appeals consent and agree to the following:

(1) The amount of any Federal _____*income*_____ tax due on any return(s) made by
                                               (Kind of tax)
or for the above taxpayer(s) for the period(s) ended __12/31/90_____

_____

may be assessed at any time on or before _____12/31/94_____ . However, if
                                                      (Expiration date)

a notice of deficiency in tax for any such period(s) is sent to the taxpayer(s) on or before that date, then the time for assessing the tax will be further extended by the number of days the assessment was previously prohibited, plus 60 days.

(2) This agreement ends on the earlier of the above expiration date or the assessment date of an increase in the above tax that reflects the final determination of tax and the final administrative appeals consideration. An assessment for one period covered by this agreement will not end this agreement for any other period it covers. Some assessments do not reflect a final determination and appeals consideration and therefore will not terminate the agreement before the expiration date. Examples are assessments of: (a) tax under a partial agreement; (b) tax in jeopardy; (c) tax to correct mathematical or clerical errors; (d) tax reported or amended returns; and (e) advance payments. In addition, unassessed payments, such as amounts treated by the Service as cash bonds and advance payments not assessed by the Service, will not terminate this agreement before the expiration date.

This agreement ends on the above expiration date regardless of any assessment for any period includible in a report to the Joint Committee on Taxation submitted under section 6405 of the Internal Revenue Code.

(3) The taxpayer(s) may file a claim for credit or refund and the Service may credit or refund the tax within 6 months after this agreement ends.

_____
(SIGNATURE INSTRUCTIONS AND SPACE FOR SIGNATURE ARE ON THE BACK OF THIS FORM)   Form **872** (Rev. 8-88)

MAKING THIS CONSENT WILL NOT DEPRIVE THE TAXPAYER(S) OF ANY APPEAL RIGHTS TO WHICH THEY WOULD OTHERWISE BE ENTITLED.

YOUR SIGNATURE HERE → *A. Taxpayer* _____   _____
                                                                       (Date signed)

SPOUSE'S SIGNATURE → _____   _____
                                                                       (Date signed)

TAXPAYER'S REPRESENTATIVE
SIGN HERE → _____   _____
                                                                       (Date signed)

CORPORATE
NAME → _____

CORPORATE   _____   _____   _____
OFFICER(S)   *(Title)*   *(Date signed)*
SIGN HERE →   _____   _____   _____
                                                  (Title)   *(Date signed)*

_____   _____
DISTRICT DIRECTOR OF INTERNAL REVENUE   REGIONAL DIRECTOR OF APPEALS

BY _____   _____
          (Signature and Title)   *(Date signed)*

Instructions

If this consent is for income tax, self-employment tax, or FICA tax on tips and is made for any year(s) for which a joint return was filed, both husband and wife must sign the original and copy of this form unless one, acting under a power of attorney, signs as agent for the other. The signatures must match the names as they appear on the front of this form.

If this consent is for gift tax and the donor and the donor's spouse elected to have gifts to third persons considered as made one-half by each, both husband and wife must sign the original and copy of this form unless one, acting under a power of attorney, signs as agent for the other. The signatures must match the names as they appear on the front of this form.

If this consent is for Chapter 41, 42, or 43 taxes involving a partnership or is for a partnership return, only one authorized partner need sign.

If this consent is for Chapter 42 taxes, a separate Form 872 should be completed for each potential disqualified person, entity, or foundation manager that may be involved in a taxable transaction during the related tax year. See Revenue Ruling 75-391, 1975-2 C.B. 446.

If you are an attorney or agent of the taxpayer(s), you may sign this consent provided the action is specifically authorized by a power of attorney. If the power of attorney was not previously filed, you must include it with this form.

If you are acting as a fiduciary (such as executor, administrator, trustee, etc.) and you sign this consent, attach Form 56, Notice Concerning Fiduciary Relationship, unless it was previously filed.

If the taxpayer is a corporation, sign this consent with the corporate name followed by the signature and title of the officer(s) authorized to sign.

Form **872** (Rev. 8-88)

Form 870. Waiver of Restrictions on Assessment.

Form **870** (Rev. February 1986)	Department of the Treasury — Internal Revenue Service **Waiver of Restrictions on Assessment and Collection of Deficiency in Tax and Acceptance of Overassessment**	Date received by Internal Revenue Service

Names and address of taxpayers *(Number, street, city or town, State, ZIP code)* A. TAX PAYER 123 TAX BLVD. Washington DC	Social security or employer identification number 000-00-0000

Increase (Decrease) in Tax and Penalties

Tax year ended	Tax	Penalties		
1990	$ 19,100	$	$ 1,000	$	$
	$	$	$	$	$
	$	$	$	$	$
	$	$	$	$	$
	$	$	$	$	$
	$	$	$	$	$
	$	$	$	$	$

Instructions

General Information

If you consent to the assessment of the deficiencies shown in this waiver, please sign and return the form in order to limit any interest charge and expedite the adjustment to your account. Your consent will not prevent you from filing a claim for refund *(after you have paid the tax)* if you later believe you are so entitled. It will not prevent us from later determining, if necessary, that you owe additional tax; nor extend the time provided by law for either action.

We have agreements with State tax agencies under which information about Federal tax, including increases or decreases, is exchanged with the States. If this change affects the amount of your State income tax, you should file the required State form.

If you later file a claim and the Service disallows it, you may file suit for refund in a district court or in the United States Claims Court, but you may not file a petition with the United States Tax Court.

We will consider this waiver a valid claim for refund or credit of any overpayment due you resulting from any decrease in tax and penalties shown above, provided you sign and file it within the period established by law for making such a claim.

Who Must Sign

If you filed jointly, both you and your spouse must sign. If this waiver is for a corporation, it should be signed with the corporation name, followed by the signatures and titles of the corporate officers authorized to sign. An attorney or agent may sign this waiver provided such action is specifically authorized by a power of attorney which, if not previously filed, must accompany this form.

If this waiver is signed by a person acting in a fiduciary capacity *(for example, an executor, administrator, or a trustee)* Form 56, Notice Concerning Fiduciary Relationship, should, unless previously filed, accompany this form.

Consent to Assessment and Collection

I consent to the immediate assessment and collection of any deficiencies *(increase in tax and penalties)* and accept any overassessment *(decrease in tax and penalties)* shown above, plus any interest provided by law. I understand that by signing this waiver, I will not be able to contest these years in the United States Tax Court, unless additional deficiencies are determined for these years.

Signatures	*a. Taxpayer*		Date
			Date
	By	Title	Date

Form 870-AD. Offer of Waiver of Restrictions.

Form **870-AD** (Rev. December 1986)	DEPARTMENT OF THE TREASURY – INTERNAL REVENUE SERVICE **OFFER OF WAIVER OF RESTRICTIONS ON ASSESSMENT AND COLLECTION OF DEFICIENCY IN TAX AND OF ACCEPTANCE OF OVERASSESSMENT**	
SYMBOLS	NAME OF TAXPAYER A. TAXpayer	SSN or EIN 000 00-0000

Pursuant to the provisions of section 6213(d) of the Internal Revenue Code of 1986, or corresponding provisions of prior internal revenue laws, the undersigned offers to waive the restrictions provided in section 6213(a) of the Internal Revenue Code of 1986, or corresponding provisions of prior internal revenue laws, and to consent to the assessment and collection of the following deficiencies with interest as provided by law. The undersigned offers also to accept the following overassessments as correct:

DEFICIENCIES (OVERASSESSMENTS)

YEAR ENDED	KIND OF TAX	TAX				
12/31/90	income	$ 10,100	$	$		
		$	$	$		
		$	$	$		
		$	$	$		
		$	$	$		
		$	$	$		

	DATE
SIGNATURE OF TAXPAYER a. Taxpayer	
SIGNATURE OF TAXPAYER	DATE
BY	TITLE	DATE

FOR INTERNAL REVENUE USE ONLY	DATE ACCEPTED FOR COMMISSIONER	SIGNATURE
	OFFICE	TITLE

(SEE REVERSE SIDE)

Form **870-AD** (Rev. 12 86)
·2/87 page 721,315

Always Check the IRS Computation of Taxes.

The IRS makes many mistakes in computations of both interest and tax liability. Always review the computations carefully and request a recomputation if the numbers do not seem correct. If you can not verify the accuracy of the recomputation, go directly to a tax professional. I have had case after case where the IRS has computed the deficiency incorrectly. In one instance, taxpayer had a large investment tax credit that was not used on the original tax return because he could not utilize the credit as he was subject to the alternative minimum tax that can not be reduced by the investment tax credit. Upon audit, the IRS increased his tax liability and therefore he could make use of the credit. The recomputation of the tax liability did not take the investment tax credit into account. Once I pointed this out, the Revenue Agent recalculated his tax and no money was due.

In another instance, the IRS adjusted the period of amortization. This reduced the amount of write off in the first year where the taxpayer originally deducted the expense in full. However, in the next two tax years taxpayer was allowed additional amortization. Upon my noticing the error the Revenue Agent issued a revised report where the refunds due in the 2nd and 3rd year erased the deficiency due in the first year.

In over 75% of the cases I have handled there have been mistakes in the recomputation of tax due or the application of interest. In one instance, the recomputation went back and forth with

6 revisions over a 3 year period. Be careful. Sometimes an adjustment in one year will mandate a favorable offset in another year that is not under audit. If you do not file a timely amended return you may lose your right to take advantage of the offset. In one case I handled, the Revenue Agent had disallowed intangible drilling costs in the year under audit as the costs were actually incurred in a later year. Taxpayer failed to file an amended return to claim these deductions in the subsequent year and lost the potential refund.

In another situation, the IRS Revenue Agent had disallowed deductions and losses generated by a tax shelter investment that they claimed were nonexistent losses as no transactions had actually taken place. The tax shelter promoters were arrested and in jail because they had taken the money invested by taxpayer. Taxpayer came to me to review the recomputation and I discovered that he had reported income in later years from these same nonexistent transactions. I asked the IRS why they had not reversed the income, if they had reversed the deductions. Their response was to credit taxpayer with a large refund instead of the six figure deficiency originally proposed.

In other situations, you may reach an agreement with appeals, but when the bill comes it does not reflect the agreed settlement. This results from an error at the computer center. In one situation, it took me over one year to resolve and I had the appeals officer's full cooperation.

The final thing to remember is that you must check all calculations made by the IRS. You should also check to confirm that the IRS has credited you with any refunds.

Always Check the Interest Computations That Are Applied to the Deficiency.

The IRS compounds interest daily. It is not a deduction for non-corporate taxpayers. Interest payable on deficiencies is 1% more than the interest paid by the government on refunds paid to you.

The IRS calculates interest at the applicable rate from the date prescribed for payment of the tax to the date the tax is actually paid. On overpayments, the IRS pays interest from the date the IRS credits the overpayment or a date within thirty days before a refund check is generated. Interest is payable on interest.

To be sure that the IRS calculates interest correctly, you should check the following:

◊ Be sure that the period for the interest accrual is correct.

◊ Be sure that the IRS has applied the correct interest rate.

◊ Be sure that the overall computation is correct.

The IRS can never forgive interest. The IRS can reduce or eliminate interest in conjunction with an offer in compromise discussed later in this book. Accordingly, it is fruitless to negotiate with the Revenue Agent to reduce or eliminate the interest.

You Should Respond to All IRS Bills With a Written Response.

After a certain period of time, the IRS will send you a bill for the amounts assessed during the audit. The first notice (see page 42) shows the assessment of tax due and adds the interest and penalties, if any. Always respond to these notices. If you can not pay immediately, let the IRS know. Establish communications. You will receive a second and third notice, normally five weeks apart before you receive a Notice of Intent to Levy (see page 43). You have 30 days after this notice to negotiate a hold on collection of your account and a related payment agreement or accept potential levy action.

Department of the Treasury
Internal Revenue Service
PHILADELPHIA, PA   19255

Date of this notice: OCT. 11, 1993
Taxpayer Identifying Number
Form: 941   Tax Period: MAR. 31, 1993

Il.....l...lIll..lIIll.l.llIll.....l.ll..l..l.lll.l.ll....ll

For assistance you may
call us at:

649-2361   LOCAL RICHMOND
1-800-829-1040   OTHER VA

Or you may write to us at
the address shown at the
left. If you write, be
sure to attach the bottom
part of this notice.

REQUEST FOR PAYMENT

                                        FEDERAL EMPLOYMENT TAX

    OUR RECORDS SHOW YOU OWE $50.87 ON YOUR RETURN FOR THE ABOVE TAX PERIOD.
A PORTION OF THE PENALTY SHOWN BELOW IS BECAUSE YOUR TAX DEPOSITS WERE NOT MADE IN
SUFFICIENT AMOUNTS BY THE DATES REQUIRED. IF YOU BELIEVE OUR RECORDS ARE NOT CORRECT,
PLEASE SEE THE INFORMATION ABOUT THE AMOUNT YOU OWE ON THE FLAP OF THE ENCLOSED ENVELOPE.

    TO AVOID ADDITIONAL PENALTY AND/OR INTEREST, PLEASE ALLOW ENOUGH MAILING TIME SO THAT WE
RECEIVE YOUR PAYMENT BY OCT. 21, 1993. MAKE YOUR CHECK OR MONEY ORDER PAYABLE TO THE
INTERNAL REVENUE SERVICE. SHOW YOUR TAXPAYER IDENTIFYING NUMBER ON YOUR PAYMENT AND MAIL IT
WITH THE BOTTOM PART OF THIS NOTICE. IF YOU BELIEVE THIS NOTICE IS NOT CORRECT, PLEASE SEE THE
INFORMATION ABOUT THE PAYMENTS YOU MADE ON THE FLAP OF THE ENCLOSED ENVELOPE.
                                     TAX STATEMENT

        TAX ON RETURN $1,101.60

        TOTAL CREDITS $1,469.29
        AMOUNT PREVIOUSLY REFUNDED TO YOU $.00
        CREDIT BALANCE $367.69-
        *PENALTY   385.56
        *INTEREST   33.00

        AMOUNT YOU OWE $50.87

THE FOLLOWING IS A LIST OF PAYMENTS WE HAVE CREDITED TO YOUR ACCOUNT FOR THE ABOVE TAX AND
TAX PERIOD:
DATE OF PAYMENT   AMOUNT   DATE OF PAYMENT   AMOUNT   DATE OF PAYMENT   AMOUNT
  SEP. 3, 1993   1,469.29

                              PENALTY AND INTEREST CHARGES

        $247.86 FILING LATE - SEE ENCLOSED NOTICE, CODE 01
        $110.16 FAILURE TO DEPOSIT/PAYMENTS MADE DIRECTLY TO IRS - SEE ENCLOSED NOTICE, CODE 43
        $27.54 PAYING LATE - SEE ENCLOSED NOTICE, CODE 07
        $33.00 INTEREST - SEE ENCLOSED NOTICE, CODE 69

To make sure that IRS employees give courteous responses and correct information to taxpayers, a second IRS employee sometimes listens in on
telephone calls.
Keep this part for your records   Overlay 6 Form 8488 (Rev. 11-87)

828 5201

P 903 805 506

28254-479-52012-1   9116

Department of the Treasury
Internal Revenue Service
PHILADELPHIA PA 19255

DATE OF NOTICE: 04-29-91   9122   CP504
TAXPAYER IDENTIFYING NUMBER:
FORM CIV PEN   TAX PERIOD 09-30-90

FOR ASSISTANCE YOU MAY CALL US AT:

l..ll..ll...l...l.l..l.ll...........l.l.ll...lll.ll.l.l..l.ll.llll

962-2590 LOCAL BALTIMORE
1-800-829-1040 D.C./OTHER MD

OR YOU MAY WRITE TO US AT THE
ADDRESS SHOWN AT THE LEFT. IF
YOU WRITE, BE SURE TO ATTACH
THE BOTTOM PART OF THIS NOTICE.

NOTICE OF INTENT TO LEVY

OUR RECORDS SHOW THAT WE HAVE PREVIOUSLY SENT YOU NOTICES BUT WE HAVE NOT RECEIVED FULL PAYMENT OF THE FEDERAL TAX LIABILITY SHOWN BELOW. THIS IS YOUR FINAL NOTICE.

A NOTICE OF FEDERAL TAX LIEN, WHICH IS A PUBLIC NOTICE THAT THERE IS A TAX LIEN AGAINST YOUR PROPERTY, MAY BE FILED AT ANY TIME TO PROTECT THE INTEREST OF THE GOVERNMENT. IF YOU DO NOT TAKE THE REQUESTED ACTION WITHIN 30 DAYS FROM THE DATE OF THIS NOTICE, WE MAY, WITHOUT FURTHER NOTICE TO YOU, LEVY UPON AND SEIZE YOUR PROPERTY AND RIGHTS TO PROPERTY. SECTION 6331 OF THE INTERNAL REVENUE CODE ALLOWS US TO SEIZE WAGES, BANK ACCOUNTS, COMMISSIONS, AND OTHER INCOME. REAL ESTATE AND PERSONAL PROPERTY SUCH AS BUSINESS ASSETS AND AUTOMOBILES MAY ALSO BE SEIZED. THE ENCLOSED PUBLICATION CONTAINS AN EXPLANATION OF THE ACTIONS WE MAY TAKE.

TO PREVENT ACTION FROM BEING TAKEN, SEND FULL PAYMENT TODAY BY CHECK OR MONEY ORDER PAYABLE TO THE INTERNAL REVENUE SERVICE. WRITE YOUR SOCIAL SECURITY NUMBER OR EMPLOYER IDENTIFICATION NUMBER ON YOUR PAYMENT. INCLUDE THE BOTTOM PART OF THIS NOTICE WITH YOUR PAYMENT SO WE CAN QUICKLY CREDIT YOUR ACCOUNT.

WE HAVE CALCULATED PENALTY AND INTEREST AMOUNTS TO THE DATE OF THIS NOTICE. IF FULL PAYMENT IS NOT RECEIVED WITHIN 10 DAYS FROM THE DATE OF THIS NOTICE, ADDITIONAL INTEREST AND PENALTIES WILL BE CHARGED AND WILL CONTINUE UNTIL THE ACCOUNT IS FULL PAID. THE FAILURE TO PAY PENALTY INCREASES FROM ONE-HALF TO ONE PERCENT.

IF YOU RECENTLY PAID THE AMOUNT DUE, OR IF YOU CANNOT PAY THIS AMOUNT IN FULL, CONTACT THE OFFICE SHOWN ABOVE TODAY.

TAX FORM: CIV PEN
TAX PERIOD: 09-30-90

BALANCE OF PRIOR ASSESSMENTS	$90,834.86
LATE PAYMENT PENALTY	$0.00
INTEREST	$524.04
TOTAL AMOUNT DUE	$91,358.90

TO MAKE SURE IRS EMPLOYEES GIVE COURTEOUS RESPONSES AND CORRECT INFORMATION TO TAXPAYERS, A SECOND EMPLOYEE SOMETIMES LISTENS IN ON TELEPHONE CALLS.
KEEP THIS PART FOR YOUR RECORDS

Always Check to be Sure That the Statute of Limitations on Assessment of Taxes Has Not Expired. If it Has Expired, the IRS Can Not Assess Additional Taxes.

In many instances the statute of limitations can be an effective tool for stopping government action when the IRS has failed to act within the required period. This is always the first issue that you must confirm when confronting any assessment.

The rule is that the IRS must assess any internal revenue tax within three years of the time you file a tax return. Failure to assess tax within this period means that the IRS can not legally collect the tax. This period of limitations applies also to the penalties and interest that the IRS is trying to collect for that tax period.

Before you pay any assessment, you should always check and be sure that the assessment of tax is timely. So, in confirming the accuracy and validity of any assessment, you must take into account any voluntary consents to extend the time for the IRS to make assessments.

A major issue in determining when the three year period starts to run deals with the issue of when the IRS considers a tax return to be filed:

◊ If a return is timely mailed, the date of the postmark or registered postmark starts the running of the period for the statute of limitations.

◊ If the due date of the tax return is on a Saturday, Sunday, or holiday, the next business day starts the running of the statute of limitations period.

◊ If you file your tax return early, the IRS will consider it filed on the due date of the tax return, not on the date filed.

◊ If you file an amended tax return, the period starts to run on the date you filed the original return, not the amended return. An amended tax return does not effect the period for the statute of limitations.

Notwithstanding the general three year period for assessments, the IRS can make some assessments at any time:

◊ If you file a false or fraudulent tax return with the intent to evade tax.

◊ If you fail to file a tax return.

In both of the situations above, the IRS may make an assessment at any time. The case may be put into collections without an assessment by proceeding in court to collect the tax. Further, there is a 6 year statute of limitations in cases involving tax returns with a 25% omission of gross income.

In many instances, the taxpayer will come to me and state that the time for assessment has passed. I will raise this issue with the Revenue Agent or the Appeals Officer and they will normally come back to me with an executed Form 872 or 872-A that was voluntarily executed by the taxpayer before I became involved in the case and which extends the period to assess taxes. This tells me that most taxpayers do not fully understand what forms they are signing and what rights they have given away.

When You Pay Taxes or Interest Make Sure You Designate What Period the Payment is to Be Applied To.

When you prepay taxes or pay an assessed amount you should always indicate by written correspondence what period you want the payment applied to. This is a very important issue. Some taxes are dischargeable in bankruptcy and other taxes are not. Obviously, if you were making a payment and bankruptcy is an option you would want your payments applied to the taxes that are not dischargeable. If you do not indicate which period the payment relates to, the IRS will apply the payments to the earliest period.

You should always request a statement of account to be sure that the IRS has credited all payments to your account. In many instances, the IRS has not credited requested refunds correctly and interest continues to run on assessed deficiencies. You should clearly mark all payments as to the period and type of tax, interest and penalty to which it should be applied. Also in many cases, taxpayers have requested a statement of account and have found erroneous assessments that they had not been aware of.

If You Are a Non-filer Go Directly to Your Nearest Tax Professional and File Your Returns With the IRS Voluntarily.

The IRS is getting more and more sophisticated in tracking those people who have not filed tax returns. The IRS estimates that there are 10 million non-filers. The IRS is spending a lot of its resources on tracking these non-filers so that they can achieve full and voluntary compliance.

If the IRS finds that you have not filed your tax returns, it may prepare them for you based on the information it has. This information normally comes from W-2's or Form 1099's for interest and dividends. It also may have records or stock or bond transactions. The problem with this is that the IRS will report your stock transactions without deducting your original cost to determine the taxable gain. They will also not take any itemized deductions that you may have. You will then have the burden to resubmit your tax returns based on the correct information.

Before contacting the IRS, you should prepare your delinquent tax returns. Then you should file each return at the appropriate service center. Each year should be filed in separate envelopes so that the IRS does not misplace any of the years. If you file voluntarily, the IRS normally makes the assessments based on your figures. Usually, the IRS does not audit delinquent tax returns on a routine basis. Then you need only deal with collection matters relating to the delinquent taxes, if any.

Many taxpayers have come to me because they have not filed their tax returns for a number of years. Upon preparing the back tax returns, I have discovered that many taxpayers do not owe any money, but have over withheld taxes and are due a refund. However, it is too late to claim the refund. Therefore, the IRS will not refund the money.

You Have Rights at the Conclusion of the Audit. Do Not Agree to the Assessment of Additional Taxes if You Wish to Fight the Revenue Agent's Determination. Be Careful What You Sign.

At the conclusion of the audit, the Revenue Agent may recommend no change to your tax return or assert a deficiency. If you agree with the Revenue Agent's report you can execute Form 870 consenting to immediate assessment of tax. This will allow you to pay the tax due and owing without excess accumulation of interest and penalties.

If you do not agree, the Revenue Agent will prepare a report. The group manager will review the report. After this time, you will receive a copy of the Revenue Agent's Report or 30 Day Letter. This letter gives you the right to appeal the case to the Regional Director of Appeals. The IRS settles over 65% of all cases at Appeals. Do not lose your right to go to the Appeals conference by consenting to immediate assessment. Many times the Revenue Agent will trick you into executing Form 870 by telling you that you have no chance of winning the case or that if you sign the form to consent to assessment you will not owe as much interest. If you are not sure if you should sign the consent, consult professional tax advice.

You Can Avoid Liability for Delinquent Taxes if You Are an Innocent Spouse Even Though You Signed a Joint Return With Your Husband or Wife.

If a husband and wife file a joint tax return, both parties assume joint and several liability. The Internal Revenue Code does provide one provision whereby the innocent spouse can escape liability even though you and your spouse have filed a joint tax return.

To use this provision, you must prove the following:

◊ The innocent spouse must have filed a joint tax return with the guilty spouse.

◊ On the joint tax return, there is an understatement of taxes of at least $500.00 and such understatement relates to the "grossly erroneous items of the other spouse."

◊ When the innocent spouse signed the return, he or she did not know and had no reason to know that there was a substantial underpayment of tax.

◊ Based on all the facts and circumstances, it would be inequitable to hold the innocent spouse liable for the guilty spouse's action. The IRS normally looks to whether the innocent spouse received a benefit over and above the normal living requirements.

Normally this defense will be successfully used in the collection process when the IRS is attempting to collect from you and you believe your spouse had the benefit of the unreported funds or the original tax savings.

You Have Rights to IRS Information.
You Need to be Aware of IRS Position on Legal
Issues Which May Impact Upon Your Tax Return.
The IRS Can Not Settle a Case, if Such
Settlement Would be Contrary to IRS Position.

The law allows all taxpayers the right to have access to records that the IRS keeps about them. The law allows an individual the right to inspect IRS records and correct any inaccuracies. You may use these rules to guarantee that the IRS collects information in civil tax cases from you rather than from other third parties.

To obtain information about the IRS the taxpayer can review the Internal Revenue Manual. This is one of the largest manuals and includes information on IRS procedures, audit criteria, how the IRS makes assessments and other pertinent IRS operating procedures. This manual will provide you with the knowledge of how IRS personnel approach a problem or issue. You may review the Internal Revenue Manual at any public reading room in either the National Office in Washington, D.C. or at any of a number of Regional IRS offices. The Internal Revenue Manual is broken down as follows:

Part I   — Administration
Part II   — Collection Procedures for Branch Offices
Part III   — Service Center Procedures
Part IV — Audit

IRS personnel must comply with the duties and responsibilities set forth in the manual. The important point to remember is
that you can obtain a better understanding of how the internal
procedures of the IRS function. You will then understand what the
Revenue Agent can and can not do in certain situations.

The IRS also puts out other technical information that you can
also have access to. The IRS issues private letter ruling to various
taxpayers on legal issues. You can not use these private letter rulings to support your position on audit as they are not binding statements of IRS policy. They apply only to the particular taxpayer requesting the information. They are good to review because they do
indicate IRS ruling positions for that period of time. If you should be
under audit, and a novel or complex legal issue comes up, you
may consider asking the Revenue Agent to request Technical Advice. This may be to your advantage if you know that there are
some private letter rulings that are favorable to you. The IRS also
issues General Counsel Memorandums. These documents set forth
IRS policy on legal issues and you can win your case if you can
find one that supports your legal position.

Many cases came across my desk when I was working for the
IRS that the IRS had argued contrary to a General Counsel Memorandum that I was aware of but taxpayer was not. If taxpayer had
been aware of the General Counsel Memorandum, the taxpayer
would have won the case on audit or on appeal.

Even if you find a favorable case, the IRS may not follow it.
The IRS issues Actions on Decisions which state which case hold-
ings they will follow and which issues they are continuing to litigate even though they have lost in court.

SURVIVAL #21 STRATEGY

Beware of Penalties. Know Which Penalties Can Be Asserted and How to Avoid Them. Penalties Can Double the Potential Liability.

Because our system of tax is voluntary, the legislature of our country has enacted penalties to enforce compliance. Normally civil penalties consist of a system of monetary fines.

A. The Civil Fraud Penalty

The IRS will assert this penalty if any part of any underpayment of tax required to be shown on a tax return is due to fraud. The penalty is equal in amount to 75% of the underpayment that is attributable to fraud. The IRS has the burden to prove whether the taxpayer is guilty of fraud. The IRS usually asserts this penalty in cases where there is a repeated pattern of understatement of income or a repeated pattern of unjustified expenses. Deliberate failure to keep records or transferring assets to the names of others to conceal income can also result in the assessment of a penalty.

The most common defenses against this penalty are that you had a lack of knowledge of the issue or that you had delegated the task to an advisor or bookkeeper. The IRS does not assert this penalty unless your activities are very extreme.

B. The Accuracy Related Penalties

There is a 20% penalty on any portion of an underpayment of tax attributable to:

◊ Negligence

◊ Substantial Understatement of Income Tax

◊ Substantial Valuation Overstatement

The penalty for negligence begins to run on the date the tax return was required to be filed and is imposed only on the portion of the underpayment that is attributable to negligence. The taxpayer carries the burden to prove that the IRS should not apply the penalty. Negligence is generally the lack of due care or failure to do what a reasonable and ordinary person would do under the circumstances. Usually the IRS asserts this penalty where there is a failure to report income or overstatement of deductions.

The penalty for substantial understatement of income tax applies when the understatement exceeds the greater of 10% of the income tax required to be shown on the tax return or $5,000. Potential penalties will depend on the amount of the understatement. The IRS will reduce this penalty if there is "substantial authority" for a position taken on the tax return. Substantial authorities include the Internal Revenue Code and Regulations, court cases, revenue rulings, revenue procedures, tax treaties, joint committee reports, legislative history, a private letter ruling directed to you, technical advice memorandum, Action on Decisions, press releases and proposed Regulations. Disclosure of a return position on an item can result in the reduction of an underpayment. Disclosure normally requires a written statement attached to the tax return.

The last penalty relating to the accuracy of the tax return is the overvaluation penalty. Generally, this penalty only applies if the valuation of the property is 200% or more of the correct value or adjusted basis. Also, if a taxpayer's excess valuation results in an underpayment of less than $5,000, no penalty will be imposed. The IRS will not assess the penalty if you can show that you had a reasonable basis for the claimed value and that you acted in good faith.

C. Frivolous Return Penalty

There is a $500 penalty when you file a frivolous return. A frivolous return is one that does not contain the necessary information on which the IRS can evaluate the return or on its face it is substantially incorrect. The IRS assesses this penalty when you file a blank tax return or you file a tax return with constitutional objections.

D. Delinquency Penalties

There are three major penalties for filing late tax returns. The IRS may impose these penalties for:

◊ Failure to timely file your tax return

◊ Failure to timely pay the tax due on the tax return

◊ Failure to timely pay an assessed tax

Where the IRS imposes a failure to timely file penalty, you will be assessed a 5% penalty per month up to a maximum of 25%. The IRS assesses the penalty on the net amount due, which is the difference between the amount required to be shown on the tax return and the amounts paid on or before the due date of the tax return. The late filing penalty starts to run from the due date of the return to the date the IRS receives the tax return.

On top of the late filing penalty, the IRS may also assess a penalty for late payment of your taxes. The late filing penalty is reduced by the amount of the late payment penalty. The late filing and late paying penalties both have a 25% cap, respectively. The IRS calculates the late payment penalty based on 2.5% per month of the amount due from the date the tax was required to be paid.

If you file your tax return late, and no tax is due, the late filing and late payment penalties would be $0 as the base to compute the penalty is the net amount of tax due. However, the Internal Revenue Code provides that if a tax return is not filed within 60 days of the due date (including extensions), the delinquency penalty shall not be less than the lesser of $100 or 100% of the amount required to be shown as tax on such tax return. The IRS can abate the penalty for reasonable cause.

If a failure to timely file a tax return is due to fraud, the amount of the late filing penalty increases from 5% to 15% for each month, up to a maximum of 75% of the net amount due.

The IRS can abate the penalties for reasonable cause. The following defenses have been successful:

◊ Death or serious physical or mental illness of a taxpayer
◊ Unavoidable absence of a taxpayer (fighting in a war or detained outside the country)
◊ Destruction of business records by fire or casualty
◊ Erroneous advice by IRS officials
◊ The tax return is filed in the wrong place

The following defenses have not been successful:

◊ Lack of funds to pay your taxes
◊ You are too busy to file
◊ You were not aware of your obligation to file
◊ You were ill, but not incapacitated
◊ Failure to estimate tax correctly so that the extension you requested was voided

There are many other situations where the IRS has abated the penalty. Many times it depends on the individual reviewing the request. I recommend at least one letter requesting abatement of the penalties. You have nothing to lose.

If You Are Under Investigation by a Special Agent, Run to Your Nearest and Most Experienced Tax Attorney. Criminal Penalties May Impose a Loss of Your Freedom by Imprisonment. You Are Entitled to All of the Constitutional Rights That You Would Have in Any Criminal Prosecution and You Must Assert Those Rights.

The IRS may impose criminal and civil penalties at the same time because the basis for each of the penalties differs. The major criminal penalties are derived from the Internal Revenue Code provision that states that "any person who willfully attempts in any manner to evade or defeat any tax . . . or the payment thereof shall, in addition to other penalties provided by law, be guilty of a felony . . ."

This provision covers taxpayers who willfully attempt to evade taxes and those who attempt to defeat payment of taxes. To be liable, the government must show a willful attempt to evade or defeat taxes and that such taxes are due and owing.

The government must first prove beyond a reasonable doubt that you failed to report your correct tax liability as a result of one of the following:

◊ An understatement or omission of income

◊ Claims of non-existent or improper deductions

◊ False allocation of income

◊ Improper claims of credit or exemption

The government need not prove the exact amount of tax that you owe, only that the amount not paid is substantial.

The government can make its case based on evidence of a specific transaction that you did not report which would generate taxable income required to be reported or it may use circumstantial evidence to prove generally that your income or deductions are not what you have claimed.

The following situations will result in an assertion by the IRS that you have evaded taxes:

◊ Double sets of books and records

◊ False entries or alterations to your books and records

◊ False invoices or documents

◊ Destruction of your books and records

◊ Concealment of assets or covering up sources of income

◊ Not keeping contemporaneous records

Carelessness or honest misunderstanding will not support a criminal penalty. Instead, the Special Agent looks for voluntary action, intentional conduct, or knowledge. A person once convicted of tax evasion may be imprisoned for up to 5 years and may be fined up to $100,000, plus the costs of prosecution.

The Internal Revenue Code also provides criminal penalties for failure to file tax returns or pay taxes as it states that "any person required under this title to pay any estimated tax or taxes, or required by this title or by regulations made under authority thereof to make a return . . . keep any records, or supply any information, who willfully fails to pay such . . . tax, make such return, keep such records, or supply such information, at the time or times required by law or regulations, shall, in addition to other penalties provided by law, be guilty of a misdemeanor. . . ."

There are four possible offenses in this statute:

◊ Willful failure to pay an estimated tax or tax

◊ Willful failure to file a tax return

◊ Willful failure to keep adequate books and records

◊ Willful failure to supply information

The fine is imprisonment for not more than one year and up to a $25,000 monetary fine.

There are also penalties of up to 3 year's imprisonment and monetary fines up to $100,000 for making false statements. The IRS can assess the penalty in the following situations:

◊ If you make a false declaration under penalty of perjury

◊ If you aid or assist in the preparation of a return or other document that is false as to a material matter

◊ If you remove or conceal property with the intent to evade or defeat collection of the tax

◊ If in connection with an Offer in Compromise, you conceal property, withhold or falsify records or make any false or misleading statement relating to your financial condition

To avoid the penalty, these defenses have been successful:

◊ Mistake or ignorance of the law

◊ Advice of counsel

◊ Taxpayer had delegated the activity and he could not readily ascertain the wrongful action

◊ Mental or physical incapacity

The first step in any good defense is to know the rules in advance. If you are aware of when the IRS can assert penalties you can take precautions to avoid those situations.

SURVIVAL #23 STRATEGY

The 10 Most Important Rules to Follow in Any Criminal Investigation.

Follow these rules in any potential criminal investigation:

1. Retain competent tax counsel immediately.

2. Limit the information which is presented.

3. Ask the Special Agent for specific questions and determine if there is an appropriate response.

4. Keep a record of all IRS meetings. Keep track of all evidence submitted to the IRS.

5. Make full and complete factual findings before presenting any information to the Special Agent. Make sure all information that you present is consistent.

6. Do not talk to the Special Agent without benefit of counsel present.

7. Do not bluff. If you do not have an answer, say so. Avoid using any explanations that you can not prove.

8. Explanations should be brief.

9. Tell your counsel the truth. He or she is bound by attorney/client privilege. To effectively represent you, your counsel must be aware of all the facts so that there are no surprises. I was once representing a taxpayer who claimed his business was closed during a particular period and therefore he had reported no income. When I attended a meeting with the Revenue Agent I discovered

that she had subpoenaed advertising records from radio stations and posters advertising the fact that the business was open. I could not respond and defend my client vigorously as I did not know all the facts.

10. Remember that **proof** is the key. Limit information to facts that you can prove.

PART TWO

8 Tips For Winning Your Case After Audit

Strategies for Winning

Introduction

Once you have the Revenue Agent's report, you must decide what to do next. Sometimes the dollar amount involved is too small to warrant the time to protest the matter. In other cases the dollar amount is large or the issue may effect a number of years, so it is necessary to continue your case and try to prevail. Whether you win or lose will depend on the strategies employed in how you choose to appeal your case. There are many different alternatives and there is no right answer. I have tried to set forth a number of principles and considerations I evaluate when going forward with a case after the audit.

Your Right to Appeal the Revenue Agent's Findings.

At the end of an audit, the Revenue Agent will write up his report with a Notice of Deficiency Waiver (see page 67). Once you sign this form, you have allowed the IRS the right to assess and collect the tax. Do not sign this Waiver if you disagree with the amount the IRS claims you owe. The IRS can not force you to sign this form. If you sign, you will lose your right to appeal the findings of the Revenue Agent administratively and your right to try the case in Tax Court.

Many times throughout the audit process, the Revenue Agent will tell taxpayers that if they prepay the tax, interest will stop accruing and therefore it is beneficial to sign the Waiver. Interest and penalties on a tax deficiency from previous years can more than double the amount due. Interest begins to run from the date the original tax was due, not the date the IRS makes the assessment. Sometimes a case can take 3 to 5 years to protest, and during such time the interest continues to accrue.

If you prepay your tax liability you lose your administrative appeal rights. Normally you will receive the Revenue Agent's report that allows you the right to appeal his findings by filing a written protest within 30 days with the Appeal Office. After the appeal or if you do not appeal within the 30 day period you will receive a Statutory Notice of Deficiency (see page 69). This is your ticket to the Tax Court. Upon receipt of the Statutory Notice of Deficiency, you have the right, within 90 days, to file a petition with the Tax Court. If you prepay your taxes, no deficiency will exist and therefore the IRS will not issue a Statutory Notice of Deficiency. Without this ticket, you have lost the right to file a petition in Tax Court.

At this point, the only way to contest the assessment is to file an administrative claim for refund after you have paid the tax. You must initiate the claim for refund. Before undertaking this course of action, you should evaluate the merits of the arguments you are presenting and determine which court, if any, has better cases to support your legal position.

In one instance, a client retained me who had prepaid the taxes. I immediately filed a claim for refund as I noticed that the IRS computation was erroneous and the taxpayer had been overcharged by $18,000. Additionally, there was another $10,000 in issue. The IRS never responded to our claim for refund. If they had responded, the case would have ended favorably without much legal fees or time expended, based on the erroneous computation. Unfortunately, there was no response and the taxpayer was forced to file a suit in the Federal District Court. Once the complaint was filed, interrogatories, answers to interrogatories and depositions were necessary. Legal fees mounted. The attorney for the government rejected two settlement proposals that I had submitted formally. It appeared that the government attorney was trying to build up taxpayer's legal fees to force a concession. Eventually I contacted an attorney in District Counsel's office who had been considering our formal settlement offers and I was able to reach an agreement. It took over 6 years to get the money back from the erroneous computation. Yes, taxpayer did receive $12,000 of interest, in addition to the $18,000, but legal fees were substantially more than they would have been if taxpayer had headed directly to Appeals.

The IRS resolves approximately 65,000 cases a year upon appeal. Do not be afraid to appeal your case. The Appeals Officer will look at the issues with a new view. The Appeals Officer will take into consideration testimony, factual issues and other hazards of litigation. He has more flexibility in settling your case than the Revenue Agent. The job of the Revenue Agent is to write up all potential revenue producing issues, while the job of the Appeals Officer is to attempt to resolve your case. A majority of my cases have been favorably resolved upon appeal.

Form 4089 (Rev.January 1983)	Department of the Treasury-Internal Revenue Service Notice of Deficiency - Waiver	Symbols E:ESP

Name, SSN or EIN, and Address of Taxpayer(s)

SSN:

Kind of Tax Income	[ ] Copy to Authorized Representative

	Deficiency
Tax Year Ended	Increase in Tax
December 31, 1991	$6,981.00

See the attached explanation for the above deficiencies

I consent to the immediate assessment and collection of the deficiencies (increase in tax and penalties) shown above, plus any interest provided by law.

Your Signature _____   _____ (Date Signed)

Spouse's Signature,
If A Joint Return
Was Filed _____   _____ (Date Signed)

Taxpayer's
Representative
Sign Here _____   _____ (Date Signed)

Corporate
Name: _____

Corporate
Officers
Sign Here _____   _____   _____
          (Signature)   (Title)   (Date Signed)

          _____   _____   _____
          (Signature)   (Title)   (Date Signed)

Note:
If you consent to the assessment of the amounts shown in this waiver, please sign and return in order to limit the accumulation of interest and expedite our bill to you. Your Consent will not prevent you from filing a claim for refund (after you have paid the tax) if you later believe you are entitled to a refund. It will not prevent us from later determining, if necessary, that you owe additional tax; nor will it extend the time provided by law for either action.
If you later file a claim and the Internal Revenue Service disallows it, you may file suit for refund in a district court or in the United States Claims Court, but you may not file a petition with the United States Tax Court.

Who Must Sign
If this waiver is for any year(s) for which you filed a

joint return, both you and your spouse must sign the original and duplicate of this form. Sign your name exactly as it appears on the return. If you are acting under power of attorney for your spouse, you may sign as agent for him or her.
For an agent or attorney acting under power of attorney, a power of attorney must be sent with this form if not previously filed.
For a person acting in a fiduciary capacity (executor, administrator, trustee), file Form 56, Notice Concerning Fiduciary Relationship, with this form if not previously filed.
For a corporation, enter the name of the corporation followed by the signature and title of the officer(s) authorized to sign.

If you agree, please sign one copy and return it; keep the other copy for your records

Form 4089 (Rev. 1-8

Department of the Treasury
Internal Revenue Service
District Director

CERTIFIED MAIL

Date of This Notice:
AUG 2 4 1993
Letter Number 531(DO)

Taxpayer Identifying Number:

Form:
1040
Tax Year Ended and Deficiency:

December 31, 1991 $6,981.00

Person to Contact:
Ms. C. Jones
Telephone Number:
(804) 771-2090

-NOTICE OF DEFICIENCY-

Dear

We have determined that you owe additional tax and other amounts as
shown for the tax year(s) identified above. This letter is your NOTICE OF
DEFICIENCY, as required by law. The enclosed waiver shows how we figured
the deficiency.

If you want to contest this determination in court before making
any payment, you have 90 days from the date of this letter (150 days
if addressed to you outside of the United States) to file a petition
with the United States Tax Court for a redetermination of the deficiency.
For a petition form, write to:

United States Tax Court
400 Second Street, NW
Washington, DC 20217

Send the completed petition form, a copy of this letter, and all
relevant statements or schedules that accompanied this letter to the
Tax Court at the same address. The court must receive it within 90
days from the above mailing date (150 days if addressed to you outside
of the United States).

The time for filing a petition with the court (90 or 150 days as
the case may be) is fixed by law. The court cannot consider your case
if the petition is filed late. If this letter is addressed to both a
husband and wife, and both want to petition the Tax Court, both must
sign and file the petition or each must file a separate, signed petition.

The Tax Court has a simplified procedure for small tax cases, when
the dispute is for $10,000 or less for any one tax year. You can get
information about this procedure, as well as a petition form you can use,
by writing to:

Clerk of the United States Tax Court
400 Second Street, NW
Washington, DC 20217

Do this promptly if you intend to file a petition with the Tax Court.

You may represent yourself before the Tax Court, or you may be represented by anyone admitted to practice before the court.

If you decide not to file a petition with the Tax Court, please sign and return the enclosed waiver form. This will permit us to assess the deficiency quickly and will limit the accumulation of interest. The enclosed envelope is for your convenience.

If you decide not to sign and return the waiver, and you do not file a petition with the Tax Court within the time limit, the law requires us to assess and bill you for the liability after 90 days from the above mailing date of this letter (150 days if this letter is addressed to you outside the United States).

If you are a "C" corporation, Section 6621(c) of the Internal Revenue Code provides that an interest rate two percent higher than the normal rate of interest be charged on deficiencies of $100,000 or more.

If you have any questions about this letter, please write to the person whose name and address are shown on this letter. If you write, please attach this letter to help us identify your account. Keep the copy for your records. Also, please include your telephone number and the most convenient time to call, so we can contact you if we need additional information.

If you prefer, you may call the IRS contact person at the telephone number shown above. If this number is outside your local calling area, there will be a long distance charge to you. You may call the IRS telephone number listed in your local directory. An IRS employee there may be able to help you, but the contact person at the address shown on this letter is most familiar with your case.

Thank you for your cooperation.

CERTIFIED MAIL
NO. 324101

Sincerely yours,

Michael P. Dolan

Acting Commissioner

District Director

Enclosures:
Copy of this letter
Statement
Envelope

SURVIVAL #25 STRATEGY

When to Go to Appeals and How to Utilize the Appeals Process to Your Benefit.

Go directly to Appeals in the following circumstances:

◊ If you do not have the funds to pay for the high cost of litigation, but you do not agree with the Revenue Agent's conclusions.

◊ If you need to stall your case as you are awaiting another court decision which will be favorable to you.

◊ You want another opportunity to settle your case and narrow the issues before going to court.

◊ You want to defer payment of the ultimate deficiency as you do not have the funds to pay the deficiency and you believe the proposed assessment is excessive.

◊ You need more time to construct your legal arguments and to compile additional evidence and factual development.

◊ Your issues impact on related cases.

◊ You plan to request attorneys fees. To get attorneys fees, when the IRS position is unreasonable, you must exhaust your administrative remedies before heading to court and therefore you can not bypass Appeals.

You should not consider going to Appeals a waste of time. It is just one more opportunity for your position to be considered.

SURVIVAL #26 STRATEGY

When NOT to Go to Appeals.

In some situations it may not be advisable to go to Appeals. You should avoid Appeals in the following circumstances:

◊ If your case involves new issues that can be raised. The Appeals Officer is more experienced than the Revenue Agent so he or she might spot other issues. The policy of the IRS is that the Appeals Officer will not reopen or raise a new issue unless the grounds for the action are substantial and the potential effect upon the tax liability is material. You may raise new issues and the Appeals Officer can consider new evidence.

◊ If your case involves fraud issues, the Appeals Officer can not consider settlement of fraud penalty cases. If the case is first docketed in Tax Court the attorney handling the case will be more sensitive to litigation issues and trying to prove the case in court.

◊ If you want to resolve the issue quickly, going to Appeals may slow down the process.

◊ If you want a binding settlement. Settlements in docketed Tax Court cases are binding. Settlements in Appeals are not binding if there has been any concealment, misrepresentation or fraud.

Draft the Protest Letter to the Appeals Officer in Such a Way That Your Position is Clearly and Completely Articulated. Include All Relevant Facts and Legal Arguments.

There is no special IRS form for the Appeal Protest Letter. You must file it in duplicate. If does need to contain the following information:

◊ Your name and address

◊ Date and symbols of the Revenue Agent's Report

◊ Tax periods and amounts protested

◊ Statement of adjustments which are protested

◊ Statement of facts

◊ Statement of law

You must submit the Appeal Protest Letter under penalties of perjury. Your Appeal Protest Letter should be complete. You have the burden to prove that the Revenue Agent made an improper determination. You should draft your response as if you are prepared to go to court. A sample letter is included on page 73.

PROTEST

I. NAME AND ADDRESS

II. TAXABLE YEARS INVOLVED

Fiscal year ended June 30, 1990
Fiscal year ended June 30, 1991

III. SCHEDULE OF FINDINGS TO WHICH EXCEPTION IS TAKEN

Exception is taken to the disallowance of taxpayer's deduction of the amount paid to Mr. and Mrs.   in 1990 and 1991 as reasonable compensation for salary or other compensation for personal services actually rendered under Section 162(a)(1) of the Internal Revenue Code of 1986, as amended ("Code") or as deferred compensation under a non-qualified retirement plan pursuant to Section 404(a)(5) of the Code.

IV. STATEMENT OF FACTS

In 1969,   founded   , a retail catalog showroom. During the critical development years,   was the principal force behind the corporation, serving as its president, chief financial officer and chairman of its board of directors. Occupying these key positions,   , through the very substantial services he rendered, was directly responsible for the growth and success of the corporation.

Under Mr.   direct supervision and control, the corporation experienced continual and substantial growth. Reflecting Mr.   outstanding ability, total sales rose from a minimal amount in 1969, the year of the corporation's founding, to   million in 1981, to   million in 1990.

This success was not achieved without sacrifice. During the early years of the corporation's development, Mr.   devoted nearly all his time to the business of the corporation. All available cash was reinvested to finance expansion and growth. Because cash was tight, Mr. and Mrs.   often waived their right to receive a full and regular salary. As a result, Mr. and Mrs.   were significantly underpaid during the first 16 years of the corporation's existence. It was not until 1986 that Mr. and Mrs.   accepted the full amount of salary. In addition to their sacrifice in salary, Mr. and Mrs.   also refused to declare dividends during these periods even though they were the sole shareholders, so as to create a reserve for expansion purposes.

The corporation experienced continued success throughout the 1980's. Under Mr. leadership during this period, sales increased more than 300%. With the coming of the 1990s, the corporation found itself in a tight cash position. When reinvested earnings became insufficient to finance further expansion and sales slipped to the point where the corporation had a tax loss, Mr.   began to search for a solution. After bids from potential buyers fell through, Mr.   spent tremendous hours personally liquidating his company. He even opened new outlets to further expedite the liquidation process. All the while, his eye was focused on reputation and customer service. Attached hereto are several articles which highlight Mr. success.

Mrs.   compensation is also at issue. Before the founding of Mrs.   was already active in business. She had worked closely with her husband in his jewelry and engraving business, and through this and other business endeavors, had developed extensive knowledge of marketing techniques. Through her prior exposures to business she had also formed an extensive contact base which   found to be invaluable.

Once   was founded, she was hired to head the company's marketing department, and to act as its vice-president. She was the driving force that monitored the daily operations and developed the direction, along with   ·, that the department's marketing policy would follow. She personally conducted the implementation of the department's policy, working seven days every week.

Mrs.   continued to work through 1992, even though she became terribly ill with diabetes. In the last year of the company, Mrs.   assisted Mr.   in the liquidation of the inventory, and was a voice of hope for the business.

Over the years, since 1969, it had been continuously noted and acknowledged that Mr. and Mrs.   were deferring their income until later years when the company would be secure. The consensus of the board, was that certain members of the corporation had been receiving compensation substantially below that being paid to executives in other businesses similarly situated. Indeed, the board recognized that Mr. and Mrs.   throughout the years, deferred receiving their full compensation in order to assist the Corporation to meet its financial obligations and, in so doing, helped to insure the solid and substantial growth that the Corporation sustained over the years. It was therefore resolved in the meetings of the board of directors in the late 1980s and 1990s that Mr. and Mrs.   would get a year-end bonus. This bonus was set yearly and was not guaranteed for the future years.

Mr.   never ceased performance of his self imposed duties, even as he advanced in

- 2 -

age. He continued to work seven days a week, from early morning to late at night. He continued to personally supervise the running of all of the stores. He made sure that budgets were made, prices were set, and the catalog was assembled. He spent at least three months per year dedicating his time and efforts to the compilation, assembly, editing and printing of the catalog which was the heart of the catalog showroom. For his duties, Mr.   anticipated that he would receive bonuses in the later years to compensate him for compensation foregone for the growth of the company. Even in the years he received a bonus, the sum of his bonus and salary were reasonable compared to that which others in his position, in similar concerns, at similar times would expect to make.

As echoed by the board of directors in the minutes of its special meetings, and in oral discussions, the purpose of the bonuses was to secure Mr. and Mrs.   services and to secure his commitment to furnish the corporation personal services for the duration of either of their lives or the life of the company and to compensate them therefore.

Finally, in 1985, Mr. and Mrs.   agreed to accept bonuses for their outstanding work in building the corporation and for their present services which required more and more time as the business grew larger and larger. Mr. and Mrs.   never retired themselves from the day-to-day operation of the business. Instead, they saw the corporation through to its end in 1992, when they personally supervised and expedited its liquidation in the face of an ever more competitive market.

In his advisory function, Mr.   had "hands on" responsibility of all aspects of the company. He reviewed budgets and accounting data. Advise on personnel relations, catalog assembly and prior development, customer relations and business negotiations were all Mr.   iob. Mr.   was the chief financial officer as well as President of the company. Mr.   made daily visits to all of the stores and in the course of these visits, he reviewed shipping operations, financial reports, sales data and anything else that would come to his attention. In general, the corporation secured important benefits from Mr.   who provided it with valuable advise and counsel based on years of substantial experience and insight. For twenty years prior to the opening of   , Mr.   was involved in the retailing market and had substantial experience in operating a retail establishment.

V.   ISSUES PRESENTED

Whether the payments made to Mr. and Mrs.   in 1990 and 1991, are properly deductible under either Section 162(a)(1) of the Code or Section 404(a)(5) of the Code.

VI.   SUMMARY OF ARGUMENT

A.   The payments made to Mr. and Mrs.   are deductible as a reasonable allowance for salaries or as other compensation for personal services actually rendered. Section

- 3 -

162(a)(1) of the Code.

B.   Alternatively, the payments made to Mr. and Mrs.   are deductible as deferred compensation under a non-qualified retirement plan. Section 404(a)(5) of the Code.

VII. ARGUMENT

A.   Section 162 Includes Among The "Ordinary and Necessary" Expenses
      Deductible By A Business, A "Reasonable Allowance For Salaries Or Other
      Compensation For Services Actually Rendered". Section 162(a)(1) of the
      Code.

In determining whether a payment is deductible under Section 162(a)(1) of the Code, the test is whether the payments are "reasonable and are in fact payments purely for services". Regs. Section 1.162-7(a). Whether the payments are a "reasonable allowance" depends upon the facts in the particular case. In general, "reasonableness" is determined by comparing the amount of compensation paid to an individual with the value of the services performed. Treas. Reg. Section 1.162-7(a)(3) provides that reasonable compensation is the amount as would be ordinarily paid for like services by like enterprises under like circumstances. The circumstances to be taken into consideration are those existing at the date when the contract for services is made. Before such a comparison can be made the amount of compensation and the services performed must be determined. Attached hereto is an analysis of compensation paid over the years to Mr. and Mrs.   . The average compensation for the years 1970 through 1984 was $65,000 for Mr.   and $24,000 for Mrs.   . The average compensation from 1970 through 1991 was $207,306 for Mr.   and $67,400 for Mrs.   . Many studies, including the "Employee Benefit and Executive Compensation Survey", published by the National Institute of Business Management, Inc., will indicate that the salaries paid on average were reasonable given the size and type of business. The Regs under Section 162 provides as follows:

> The form or method of fixing compensation is not decisive as to
> deductibility. While any form of contingent compensation invites scrutiny
> as a possible distribution of earnings of the enterprise, it does not follow that
> payments on a contingent basis are to be treated fundamentally on any basis
> different from that applying to compensation at a flat rate. Generally
> speaking, if contingent compensation is paid pursuant to a free bargain
> between the employer and the individual made before the services are
> rendered, not influenced by any consideration on the part of the employer
> other than that of securing on fair and advantageous terms the services of the
> individual, it should be allowed as a deduction even though on the actual
> working out of the contract it may prove to be greater than the amount
> which would be ordinarily paid.

See Also, Pepsi-Cola Bottling co., Inc. v. Commissioner, 61 T.C. 564, 568 (1974).

- 4 -

The amounts paid were not influenced by any consideration on the part of the employer other than that of securing, on fair and advantageous terms, the services of Mr. and Mrs.

The important point is that the form or method of fixing compensation is not decisive. Regulations Section 1.162-7(b)(2). If the compensation set is reasonable, it will be allowed as a deduction even though it may prove to be greater than the amount which would ordinarily be paid. Id. Therefore, if pursuant to the comparison discussed above, it is determined that the compensation is reasonable, it cannot later be challenged.

To determine "reasonableness", the amount of compensation, must be compared with the value of the services actually performed.

During the years of Mr.   employment, he performed various services of an obviously substantial nature. As a full-time employee and chairman of the board, Mr.   ran the company in no uncertain terms. As founder of the corporation, Mr.   retained responsibility for its current operations and future direction until the company's liquidation in 1992.

Mrs.   was in charge of the marketing department and performed services through 1991. In 1992, she assisted in the liquidation of the company and her contribution has always been significant.

Once the amount of compensation has been determined and the services actually rendered have been identified, the court must make the comparison and render a decision on reasonableness. In the course of rendering decisions on the issue, the courts have relied on numerous different factors. An often cited list of pertinent facts and circumstances was enumerated by the Tax Court in Mayson Mfg. Co. v. Commissioner, [49-2 USTC ¶9467], 178 F.2d 115 (6th Cir. 1949). See also Estate of Wallace, et. al. v. C.I.R., 95 T.C. 37 (1990); Denison Poultry and Egg Co. v. U.S., [83-1 USTC Para. 9360] (N.D. Tex. 1982). In Mayson, the Court considered the following factors relevant:

     i.   the employee's qualifications;

     ii.   the nature extent and scope of the employee's work;

     iii.   the size and complexities of the business;

     iv.   a comparison of salaries paid with the gross income and the net income;

     v.   the prevailing general economic conditions;

vi.   comparison of salaries with distribution to
       stockholders;

vii.   the prevailing rates of compensation for
       comparable positions in comparable concerns;

viii. the salary policy of the taxpayer as to all
       employees; and

ix.   in the case of small corporations with a
       limited number of officers, the amount of
       compensation paid to the particular employee
       in previous years.
                       Id. at 116.

An additional issue of reasonableness is raised when compensation is paid to a shareholder-officer of a closely-held corporation. The courts have given lengthy consideration to the employee-shareholder's contribution to the business enterprise. See e.g., Laure v. Commissioner, 70 T.C. 1087, 1088-1091 (1978). In the present case, the employees-shareholders whose compensation is in question, were the founders and sole shareholders of the corporate employer.

Finally, Section 162 requires that an expense be "ordinary and necessary." A necessary expense is one that is appropriate or helpful to taxpayer's business and there is no requirement that it must be essential. Fouke Fur Company v. Bookwalter, 261 F.Supp. 367 (E.D. Missouri 1966).

1. Mr. _____ compensation was both reasonable and necessary.

From the date of its founding, the corporation has employed Mr.   as its president, chief financial officer and chairman of its board of directors. The valuable services rendered by Mr.   during the pre-1985 years, as well as the post-1985 years, generally consisted of supervising the overall conduct of the business. In essence, Mr.
        was the guiding force behind the corporation. He was responsible for all major decisions made on a day-to-day basis, as well as decisions made concerning the future course of business operations. Mr.   was personally involved with financial issues, sales, production, inventories, personnel management, and future planning. In sum, Mr.
        "ran" the corporation. At its peak, the corporation employed over 500 employees.

Under Mr.   guidance and control, the corporation experienced expansion and success. During the 1970's to early 1980's, sales were approximately $1 Million to $2 Million. By 1981, under Mr.   leadership, sales had grown to over $4 Million annually. By 1988, under the continued leadership of Mr.   , sales had increased

- 6 -

approximately 300% to an annual total of $16 Million.

It was recognized that the past success of the corporation was due in large part to Mr.   contributions. It was upon this proven record that the compensation was set. It was clear to those in control of the corporation that Mr.   contributions were invaluable.

Mr.   's qualifications were of a very high caliber. During the years 1949-1969 (prior to the formation of   .), Mr.   acquired invaluable experience in the retailing of jewelry and gift related products. The substantial business contacts made by Mr.   during those years also increased his value to the corporation. He was member of a key group of similarly situated catalog retail establishments in which valuable business insights were gained. In addition to the foregoing, Mr.   inherent business judgment and eye for spotting and developing new markets established the high caliber of his qualifications. Therefore, the compensation package provided to Mr.   for services as a full-time employee, is reasonable given the value of Mr.   contribution to the company.

The total amount of compensation varied from year to year based on the amount Mr. and Mrs.   decided to defer for the benefit of the company. In 1970 no compensation was received. While in later years, Mr. and Mrs.   received bonuses based on the success of the business. On an average, using the available numbers, their average compensation is reasonable in regard to others in their position.

The compensation received by Mr.   for 1990 and 1991 is reasonable for the following reasons:

i.   Due to his experience, business contacts, and inherent abilities, Mr.   was highly qualified to fill the positions of president and chairman of the board of directors;

ii. Due to his qualifications, Mr.   was an invaluable asset to the corporation;

iii. The scope and extent of the services actually rendered by Mr.   to the corporation were substantial;

iv. The compensation paid to Mr.   during the years in question did not constitute a substantial salary increase; and

v.   Given the capital requirements of the business in question and the conservative level of compensation actually set, the payments cannot be construed as a distribution of earnings and profits.

From the standpoint of   , there were two distinct, yet interrelated

- 7 -

reasons for entering into the contract:

i.   to secure the services of Mr.   as president and chairman of the board and to adequately compensate him for those valuable services; and

ii.   to secure Mr.   commitment to provide consulting and advisory services regarding the sale and liquidation of the business.

The Tax Court discussed this issue in the case of Shotmeyer v. Commissioner, 40 T.C.M. 589 (1980). In Shotmeyer, the issue was whether the payments made by Shotmeyer Bros. Petroleum Corp. (the "corporation") to Henry Shotmeyer ("Shotmeyer") were deductible as reasonable compensation under Section 162(a)(1) of the Code. As president and sole shareholder of the corporation, Shotmeyer set the level of his own compensation. During the years in question, Shotmeyer had turned over much of the day-to-day operations of the corporation to his two sons. During the three years in question, Shotmeyer had spent 14 of the 36 months with his wife at their Florida condominium. Shotmeyer did remain in continual contact with the corporation and remained responsible for most major business decisions. Prior to 1973 (the first year in question), Shotmeyer's salary was $48,362. In 1973, 1974 and 1975, Shotmeyer's salary was $137,225, $176,900 and $136,900, respectively.

The Service challenged the deduction by the corporation for these payments to Shotmeyer. The Service based its claim on the facts that the corporation has never declared or paid a dividend and that Shotmeyer's salary has substantially increased without a concurrent increase in his duties. Claiming, in fact, that Shotmeyer's corporate duties had been reduced and for the most part assumed by his sons, the Service characterized the case as involving an individual who helped found a business, made major contributions to its growth and success, but during the years in issue had become semi-retired.

After giving careful consideration to the services actually rendered by Shotmeyer during 1973-1975 and after considering the capital needs of the corporation, the Tax Court found the payments to Shotmeyer "reasonable" and, therefore, fully deductible by the corporation under §162(a)(1). Relying on the evidence of the corporation's need for capital and the fact that Shotmeyer had been under compensated in the past, the Court reasoned, "the substantial increase in salary does not support respondent's position and the prior compensation level is not indicative of a reasonable compensation for Mr. Shotmeyer." Id. at 594.

The present case is similar to Shotmeyer in many respects. Both cases involve a president of a closely held corporation. In both cases, the employee whose compensation is in question was largely responsible for the success of the business. There is evidence in both cases that the employee had formerly been underpaid. In both cases, that employee was nearly invaluable. Notwithstanding the similarities between this case and Shotmeyer, the <u>Shotmeyer</u> case presented the Court with a more difficult set of facts. In <u>Shotmeyer</u>, the employee had received a substantial salary increase while at the same time he was relieved of his day-to-day corporate duties. In this case, Mr.   did not receive a similar increase. In fact, Mr.   s duties took much more of his time as the economy worsened and he attempted to sell or liquidate his business.

Clearly, the services provided by Mr.   were of benefit to the corporation since Mr   possessed valuable experience and inherent abilities as the founder, president and chairman of the board of the corporation. Surely his many years of experience and business contacts, along with his demonstrated abilities, were extremely valuable to the corporation. The services provided certainly support the compensation Mr.   received for the years in issue.

2. Mrs.   compensation was both reasonable and necessary.

The factors considered by the courts in reaching a decision on the reasonableness of compensation were discussed previously. It was there established that Mr. significant experience made him a valuable asset. The business contacts he made and his inherent ability to spot new markets were of continuing value to the corporation. Mr. ; ability as a businessman has been demonstrated by the growth and expansion the corporation enjoyed under his leadership.

income also is in question. Mrs.   as an employee stockholder, must meet the same burden established above for employee-stockholders.

Before the founding of   , Mrs.   was already active in business. She had worked closely with her husband in his jewelry and engraving business, and through this and other business endeavors, had developed extensive knowledge of marketing techniques. Through her prior exposures to business she had also formed an extensive contact base which   . found to be invaluable.

Once   was founded, she was hired to head the company's marketing department. She was the driving force that monitored the daily operations and developed the direction, along with Mr.   , that the department's marketing policy would follow. She personally conducted the implementation of the department's policy, working seven days every week.

The compensation received by   for 1990 and 1991 is reasonable for the following reasons:

   i.   Due to her experience, business contacts, and inherent abilities,
          Mrs.   was highly qualified to fill the positions of vice-president

and head of marketing;

ii.   Due to her qualifications, Mrs.   was an invaluable asset to the
        corporation;

iii.   The scope and extent of the services actually rendered by Mrs.
        to the corporation were substantial;

iv.   The compensation paid to Mrs.   during the years in question
        did not represent a substantial salary increase; and

v.   Given the capital requirements of the business in question and the
        conservative level of compensation actually set, the payments
        cannot be construed as a distribution of earnings and profits.

Clearly, the services provided by Mrs.   were of benefit to the corporation since
Mrs.   possessed valuable experience and inherent abilities as the vice president and the
head of marketing of the corporation. Surely her many years of experience and business
contacts, along with her demonstrated abilities, were extremely valuable to the corporation.
The services provided certainly support the compensation Mrs.   received for the years
in issue. Further, we hereby incorporate the argument in A.1., above, regarding
Shotmeyer, into this section.

            3. The Payments To Mr. and Mrs.   Were Not Dividend
                Declarations.

It must be conceded, however, that the fact that the corporation is closely held, like
that in Shotmeyer, should not be dismissed lightly. As stated by the Tax Court, "[w]hen
the case involves a closely held corporation where the controlling shareholders-executives
set their own compensation as executives, the reasonableness of such compensation
necessitates our close scrutiny in order to determine if the payment of such alleged
compensation is not, in fact, a distribution of corporate profits." Miles-Conley Co. v.
Commissioner [49-1 USTC P 9245], 173 F.2d 958, 960 (4th Cir. 1979), aff'g. [Dec. 16,
368] 10 T.C. 754 (1948). If a corporation is closely held and its officers are shareholders,
and the corporation is successful but has paid no dividends, the Service may argue that part
of the total compensation is actually a dividend.

In the present case,   has not paid dividends since its incorporation
in 1969. It should be noted, however, that while the absence of dividends may prompt
close scrutiny, "it should not deprive compensation demonstrated to be reasonable under
all of the circumstances of the status of reasonableness." Edwin's Inc. v. United States,
501 F.2d 675, 677 (7th Cir. 1974) (at footnote 5); See Also, Laure v. Commissioner, 70
T.C. 1087, 1098 (1978) ("We doubt that section 162(a)(1) was intended to permit the

Commissioner or the courts to so sit in judgment over whether dividends should be paid in lieu of reasonable compensation to employee-shareholders.") The Internal Revenue Service itself has refused to adopt an "automatic dividend" rule. See Rev. Rul. 79-8, 1979-1 C.B. 97.

If the corporation can demonstrate proper business reasons for not declaring dividends, the absence of dividends, even in a closely held corporation, will not weigh in favor of a finding of unreasonableness. Neils v. Commissioner, T.C. Memo 1982-173. In the present case,   . had more than adequate business reasons for not declaring dividends. During the development years, all available   nings were reinvested into the corporation so as to create a reserve for expansion purposes. That earnings were not available for distribution during the period 1969 to 1985 is evidenced by the fact that those in control of the corporation (including Mr. and Mrs.   ) received nominal salaries during those years. Cash remained tight during the years 1969 to 1985. In order to finance current operations, the corporation found it necessary to sometimes obtain loans.

In the 1980s, the corporation expanded into new locations. During the years 1969 to 1984, net profits were used to finance the expansion of the business (including growing inventories). For these reasons, dividends were not declared. Given the foregoing, the absence of dividends should not weigh in favor of unreasonableness.

B.   The Payments Made To Mr. And Mrs.   Are Deductible As Deferred Compensation Under A Non-Qualified Retirement Plan. Section 404(a)(5) of the Code.

As fully set forth in the Statement of Facts, there was an implied oral agreement with the company, that Mr.   services as president and chairman of the board would continue as long as Mr.   remained employed on a full-time basis and would continue to provide his guidance and business expertise to the corporation on a day-to-day basis. For these services, Mr.   expected a yearly salary plus a bonus once the company gained financial security.

Pursuant to the understanding of the parties, part of the total compensation to be paid Mr.   in consideration for his services as president and chairman of the board was to be deferred until after the corporation was in a secure financial position. The deductibility of such deferred compensation payments is governed by Section 404(a) of the Code. That Section provides for a deduction by an employer for deferred compensation paid to a cash basis employee in the year of actual payment rather than the year(s) in which the services were rendered, even if the employer is an accrual basis taxpayer. Regs. Section 1.404(a)-1(c).

With regard to the payments in question, it is the position of the Service that Section

- 11 -

404(a) and (b) of the Code and the regulations thereunder permit a deduction for payments made pursuant to a plan or method of deferred compensation if such a plan involves an agreement between the employer and employee whereby the employee gives up some portion of present compensation in exchange of the employer's promise to pay a deferred benefit some time in the future.

> [I]f compensation is paid. . . on account of an employee under a plan deferring the receipt of such compensation, such . . . compensation shall not be deductible under this chapter; but if they would otherwise be deductible, they shall be deductible under this Section. . . .(5) . . . in the taxable year in which an amount attributable to the contribution is includible in the gross income of employees participating in the plan . . . Section 404(a)(5) of the Code.

In this case, given the questions of deferment of compensation and reasonableness of income, there are two requirements for deductibility under Section 404(a) that must be met. They are:

i.   that the payments be made "under a plan deferring the receipt of such compensation"; and

ii. that the payments satisfy the conditions of Section 162 of the Code.

It is not difficult to satisfy the "plan" requirement. Section 404(b) of the Code states that it is not necessary to have an actual plan. If "the method of employer . . . compensation has the effect of a . . . pension . . . or annuity plan, or other plan deferring the receipt of compensation, subsection (a) [of section 404] shall apply as if there were such a plan." Section 404(b) of the Code.

The method of compensation provided by the company effectively indicates a bonus for Mr   services in building up the company. But for his efforts, sales would not have increased from $4,000,000 in 1981 to $16,000,000 in 1988, and the business could not have expanded without retention of capital. These bonuses could not be paid until well after the company had been built up. Furthermore, it is clear from the attached analysis of yearly compensation that the plan was intended to defer a portion of compensation. Therefore, the requirements of §404 (a) have been met.

Since arguments regarding §162 were made in prior sections, they are omitted in text from this section, but fully incorporated through this reference. Given that the employment compensation package satisfies both §404 (a) (5) and §162 (a) (1) of the Internal Revenue Code, we believe it proper to judge the package, and all matters relating to it, to be in accord with the Internal Revenue Code, the case law, and the position of the Internal Revenue Service.

VII.   CONCLUSION

Mr. and Mrs   did more than contribute to the success of   . They sacrificed immediate financial gain so as to guarantee a future for the corporation they created. Further, they sacrificed their own time and efforts for the same cause.

In later years, when the company had gained financial security, Mr. and Mrs.   , with the blessing of the balance of the board of directors, elected to receive some of the compensation they had deferred from previous years. The medium of choice was bonuses. These bonuses were reasonable and necessary. as shown above. Without Mr. and Mrs.   , and their sacrifice of time and wages,   . would have never succeeded. Indeed, it would have never been formed.

For these reasons, and those stated above in other sections, fairness and logic dictate that the deferred compensation should be held to be neither excessive nor unreasonable. Additionally, the bonuses should not be reclassified as dividends. They should be found to be ordinary and necessary business expenses, the deductibility of which should not be disallowed.

We come before you to offer this information with hope that you will agree with our position. We therefore request that this cast by removed from all current and any future scrutiny.

The Key to Winning Your Case in Appeals is to Be Prepared.

The Appeals Officer does not prepare his own case so you have the advantage in being better prepared. The purpose of the Appeals conference is to focus on the issues and discuss strategies for settlement.

To use the Appeals conference to your benefit submit all evidence including third party affidavits, expert reports, charts or other data relevant to your case. All statements made by you or your representative are admissible for consideration by the Appeals Officer. Legal arguments should all be in writing and should be based on current IRS position.

Before you attend the Appeals conference you should do the following:

◊ Know all your facts and double check them

◊ Obtain and organize all books and records and other evidence

◊ Be able to **prove** all factual arguments

◊ Anticipate and be able to respond to all the IRS arguments

◊ Obtain new evidence such as appraisal reports, expert testimony or affidavits

◊ Use a black book

◊ Be fully prepared

◊ Formulate a number of proposals for settlement

If you take the above steps, in most cases your appeal will turn out favorably. At the minimum, perhaps some of the issues raised in the audit can be resolved.

Think Like the Appeals Officer. Provide a Basis for the Settlement by the Evidence and Arguments You Submit.

The Appeals Officer will ordinarily give consideration to an offer to settle a tax controversy on a basis that reflects the relative merits of opposing views in light of the hazards of litigation that would exist if the case went to court.

The Appeals Officer will determine what a court might decide on similar facts that the taxpayer can prove. The Appeals Officer will also evaluate the effect of any testimony and the expected interpretation of the law on the issue. He will take into account the following issues:

◊ Probative value of the evidence

◊ Credibility of the taxpayer as a witness

◊ Availability of other witnesses

◊ Ability of the taxpayer to satisfy the burden of proof

◊ Doubt as to the facts or the law on the issues

The Appeals Officer can not enter into a nuisance settlement. He can not settle to avoid litigation if he knows that he can **not** litigate the issue because it would be contrary to IRS policy or he knows that the IRS position can not be sustained. In those cases the Appeals Officer should concede the case.

If you can not resolve a legal issue where the law is unclear, you can request Technical Advice from the National Office. This is a system to provide guidance on internal revenue laws, statutes and regulations and is normally used where there are inconsistent IRS positions or novel legal issues involved. Technical Advice is binding so if it is adverse, your case will be headed for litigation.

Be Careful in Executing a Closing Agreement. Understand What You Are Agreeing to in Advance. A Closing Agreement is a Binding Legal Document Like Any Other Binding Contract.

A closing agreement can affect the tax liability of the same taxpayer for other years or the tax liability of a related party. To be sure that the IRS does not reopen the same issue in a later year or for a related taxpayer and a different result is reached you can negotiate the following:

◊ You can request that the Appeals Officer take jurisdiction over later years if you have already filed your tax returns. The Appeals Officer can make all adjustments in accordance with the proposed settlement.

◊ If your settlement results in an overpayment in a later year, you can file a claim for refund and use these funds to offset the deficiency. For example, if the IRS disallows a loss you took in the first year because the following year was the proper time for the deduction, you can file a claim for refund for the later year. Be alert and make sure that you file your claim for refund before the statute of limitations expire.

◊ You can request a settlement statement from the IRS. This statement sets forth IRS position on certain issues that are resolved in settlement. Usually you can use this in conjunction with issues that may change yearly based on the facts and circumstances. You can use this statement in later years if you are audited again, although it is not binding.

◊ You can request a closing agreement where the settlement in-volves multiple issues and the tax impact is material. In one situation I represented a taxpayer who had reached a settle-ment on the deductions related to his yachting business. He was reaudited and the case started all over again because his previous attorney had not requested a closing agreement. Luckily, I knew the attorney for the government that had en-tered into the first settlement and I requested that the attorney contact the new Revenue Agent to explain the prior settle-ment. This was a successful approach and the case was closed without adjustment.

There are five different options for settlement agreements. You should execute all of these agreements with care:

◊ Waiver on Restrictions of Assessment (Form 870) where the taxpayer agrees on the audit level to concede certain issues
◊ Appeals Waiver Form (Form 870 AD)
◊ Closing Agreement (Form 866)
◊ Collateral Agreement which sets forth the settlement position
◊ Stipulated Decision which is filed in Tax Court

The IRS uses the Form 870, Waiver on Restrictions of Assess-ment, when a mutual settlement is not involved. The IRS uses it for taxpayer concessions on the audit level. Once you execute this form you can not go to Tax Court, you can only file a claim for a refund after you have paid the liability. The IRS uses the Form 870 AD for mutual concessions on the Appeals level. The Form 870 AD pledges that there will not be a reopening of the case and the IRS will not make any additional assessments. You have also waived your right to file a claim for refund.

The Collateral Agreement is not a binding agreement. It solely expresses the agreement of the parties.

The Closing Agreement on the other hand, is final and bind-ing. Normally the Appeals Officer will not give you a closing

agreement, but you can request it in cases that involve a continuing issue that has a material impact on your taxes. You must also
show the IRS that it will have no adverse impact on the government. You can use this agreement even if there is no deficiency.
You will need court approval if your case is docketed (see page
93).

The IRS uses a Closing Agreement in the following instances:

◊ The fiduciary of an estate wants to be discharged by the
  Probate Court.

◊ A liquidating company wants to wind up its affairs.

◊ The taxpayer wants to fix a determination of cost, fair market
  value or other factual question as of a past date.

◊ The taxpayer wants to fix a determination of gross income,
  deduction, loss, depreciation, or year of deduction.

Be sure that you read the Closing Agreement carefully and
that it states what your agreement was with the IRS. Be sure to
request one if you have a continuing issue.

Form **866** (Rev. July 1981)	Department of the Treasury — Internal Revenue Service **Agreement as to Final Determination of Tax Liability**

(Complete three copies of this form)

Under Section 7121 of the Internal Revenue Code, **A. TAX PAYER, 123 TAX BLVD, 000-00-000C**
(Taxpayer's name, address, and identifying number)

and the Commissioner of Internal Revenue agree that the liability of the above taxpayer for the taxable periods and kinds of tax listed in this agreement is as follows: (The applicability or inapplicability of interest or penalties, including additions to tax or additional amounts authorized by Subchapter A of Chapter 68 of the Code, is not determined except as provided in this agreement.)

Taxable Period	Kind of Tax or Penalty	Chapter Number and Subchapter Letter of Internal Revenue Code	Total Tax Liability for Period
1991	1040 income		10,000

This agreement is final and conclusive except:

    (1) the liability it relates to may be reopened in the event of fraud, malfeasance, or misrepresentation of material fact and

    (2) it is subject to the Internal Revenue Code sections that expressly provide that effect be given to their provisions notwithstanding any other law or
        rule of law except Code section 7122.

    By signing this agreement, the above parties certify they have read and agreed to its terms.

Your signature **A Taxpayer**   Date signed _____

Spouse's signature *(If a joint return was filed)* _____   Date signed _____

Signature of taxpayer's representative _____   Date signed _____

Taxpayer *(other than individual)* _____

    By _____   Date signed _____

    Title _____

Commissioner of Internal Revenue

    By _____   Date signed _____

    Title _____

Part 1 — Original   (See back)   Form **866** (Rev. 7-81)

Be Certain to Take Your Case to the Court Which Will Result in Winning Your Case.

There are two ways of taking the IRS to court. Before a taxpayer proceeds, it is necessary in most instances to consult an attorney. The choice of which court ultimately hears your case can effect many issues regarding the final outcome of your battle.

A. The Refund Procedure

A taxpayer has an option to pay the full amount of the deficiency and then sue the government for a refund of the amount you believe the government has wrongfully assessed and collected. Only 5% of all tax cases use this method. Obviously, the disadvantage to this procedure is that you must prepay amounts claimed by the IRS to be due.

The first step is to file a claim for refund. The Internal Revenue Code provides the rules for filing the claim for refund. First you must determine the amount of the overpayment and then file the claim for refund (normally you can use a Form 1040X). You must file the claim for refund within 3 years of the date you filed the original tax return for the period in issue or two years from the date the tax is paid, whichever is later. In the claim for refund you must set forth in detail the facts upon which the claim is based. If the IRS denies your claim or you receive no response within 6 months you may file a suit for refund based on the same issues raised in the original claim.

Taxpayers can file a suit for refund in the US Claims Court or appropriate Federal District Court. To determine which court is more appropriate, taxpayer must examine which court has the most favorable law on the issues involved in their case.

To prevail in a refund claim, you must prove that the assessment and collection of tax was erroneous and the correct tax for such taxable year. You have the right to a jury trial in the Federal District Court, but not in the US Claims Court.

The disadvantage to a claim in the Federal District Court is that the whole tax return is in issue since you must prove the correct amount of the tax for that period. The attorney for the government can raise new issues as offsets to the claimed refund and you must prove that you are entitled to the claimed refund.

Why would you choose a suit for refund?

◊ The case law in one court is more favorable to your legal position.

◊ The case involves an employment tax issue and the Tax Court does not have authority to hear the case.

◊ You would prefer a jury trial to evaluate factual testimony.

B. The Tax Court

You always have the alternative to file your case in the Tax Court, without paying the tax in issue. The suit will be for a redetermination of the amount of the deficiency the IRS claims is due. Taxpayers file over 95% of all tax cases in the Tax Court. Unlike a refund suit, you do not have to prove the correct amount of tax due. You need only prove that the determination by the IRS is invalid.

Any previous findings by the government are irrelevant. You may use approximations and testimony to prove that the deficiency is excessive or incorrect. The Tax Court has its own rules of practice and procedure. These rules do not allow discovery to the same extent as in the Federal District Court or US Claims Court.

In either forum, the court conducts a complete review of the case and does not rely on the IRS administrative record. In either court, the assessment or determination of the IRS is presumed to be correct. The taxpayer has the burden to prove otherwise.

PART THREE

What Can You Do if You Can Not Afford to Pay the IRS?

9 Tips to Survive the IRS Attempt to Collect Taxes When You Can Not Afford to Pay

Strategies for Winning

Introduction

Unfortunately most taxpayers call me when the IRS is about to levy their wages or their bank accounts. The situation is out of control and the only way I can help them is to get the situation under control by releasing the levy and explaining to the taxpayer their options in satisfying the liability. Taxpayers do have many options but the IRS does not always outline the possibilities to taxpayers and does not always assist them in finding the best alternative for their situation. Remember that the Revenue Officer's job is to collect the most amount of taxes. You must affirmatively request certain options or else you will not obtain the best terms for you. You can not deal with the Revenue Officer without full knowledge of your rights and options that are available to you. I am normally involved in 2 or 3 cases a week where the IRS **erroneously** levies a taxpayer that has a valid hold placed on collection of his account. You are dealing with a collection agent when you are dealing with the Revenue Officer.

Know Who You Are Dealing With and How the IRS Organizes the Collection Function. Then, if Something Goes Wrong, You Know Who to Call to Resolve the Issue.

An individual working for the Automated Collection System (ACS) is normally the first individual you will deal with. ACS is located in each of the Service Centers where you file your tax returns. Usually ACS will receive your case after you receive the first 2 payment due notices.

Normally ACS will do the following:

◊ An IRS employee will make telephone contact with you to demand payment.

◊ An IRS employee will search for your assets.

◊ An IRS employee will handle your taxpayer correspondence and make adjustments to your account if you send payment.

◊ An IRS employee will place a hold on collection of your account or respond to inquiries regarding liens and levies.

After the case leaves ACS, a Revenue Officer takes over the case. The Revenue Officer has the power to collect tax, file Notices of Liens, serve levies, seize and sell real estate and personal property and negotiate installment agreements or enter into Offers in Compromise.

I find it much easier to work out an arrangement with the Revenue Officer than with ACS as in most instances they will work with you in reaching an arrangement and closing a case. In many instances, I have asked the IRS to place a hold on collection of an account and the Revenue Officer has agreed. Later ACS will go into the account and manually release the hold on collection so I have to start all over. It is very confusing to be dealing with two parts of the IRS.

SURVIVAL #33 STRATEGY

You Will Receive a Number of Different Notices. Always Respond to Each Notice and Know How Much Longer Before a Potential Levy Will Be Placed on Your Assets. This Knowledge Will Give You Time to Work Out Financial Arrangements to Ultimately Reach an Agreement With the IRS.

The first notice you will receive is a Notice of Assessment and Demand for payment within 10 days. Five weeks later you will receive a follow up balance due notice called the Notice of Unpaid Tax. This notice will include a late payment penalty addition and will request payment within 10 days to avoid additional interest and penalties. The IRS mails a second follow up notice 5 weeks after the first notice and it is a Notice of Overdue Tax. The third notice is a follow up balance due notice entitled Urgent Payment Required. This notice is also sent at the 5 week interval. The IRS sends the Final Notice of Intent to Levy 5 weeks after the last notice (see pages 42 and 43) and tells you that you have 30 days before the IRS will begin to levy your assets. The IRS sends these notices to you even though there may be a hold placed on collection of your account. They are computer generated so they are forwarded even when there is no formal collection activity going on.

Always respond to an IRS notice. If you can not afford to pay, let them know. If you can pay in the future, but not at the present time, write a letter to them so stating.

ACS is very difficult to deal with. ACS will automatically issue liens and levies. Time after time they have completed collection action when there has been a hold on taxpayer's account. You should always try to have the case transferred to a field office if possible. If your case is extremely complex or involves large amounts of money, ACS will transfer it to a Revenue Officer. The taxpayer must request the transfer in writing and the request should set forth the fact that your collection issues are unusually complex.

How To Minimize the Impact of a Federal Tax Lien.

Before filing a Notice of Federal Tax Lien (see page 107), it is the IRS policy to contact the taxpayer to determine whether filing the lien will adversely affect the taxpayer's ability to pay and therefore will adversely affect the collection of the tax. The Notice of Federal Tax Lien is not mandatory, but the IRS does place the lien, in most situations. A lien is **not** a levy. It is **not** an action to seize your property. It is notice to all potential creditors that the IRS is in line for your assets. A Notice of Federal Tax Lien must be filed prior to any levy action on property held by the taxpayer or prior to putting a taxpayer's account in the uncollectable status if the amount owed is over $2,000.

The IRS will normally file the lien if:

◊ There is a threat of adverse creditor action.

◊ There is a threat of insolvency.

◊ An asset transfer is imminent.

◊ Collection is in jeopardy.

◊ You have agreed to an installment agreement.

The lien is a claim or charge on property for a debt repayment. A lien does not transfer property. The IRS can only transfer your property by levy or seizure. After the IRS files the lien, the IRS issues the Notice of Intent to Levy, and after 30 days have passed, then the IRS can levy and seize your property.

To have a valid lien, you need to have an assessment, demand and nonpayment. The lien continues in place until you satisfy the liability or it becomes unenforceable because of lapse of time. The IRS needs to enforce the lien by collection within 6 years after assessment, unless refiled. You can voluntarily extend the period for collection.

The tax lien attaches to all of your real and personal property. The government has the same rights to the property as you have. Liens also attach to after acquired property, but it will not attach to property transferred before the assessment date if the transfer was a bona fide transfer. There are no exemptions from the federal tax lien.

Once the lien is in place, it makes it virtually impossible to get financing to pay your taxes. If you decide to sell your house and the proceeds will not be enough to satisfy the tax liability in full, you have a common problem. Nevertheless, there are several options. The first step should be to contact the Revenue Officer who filed the tax lien in the first place.

One of my clients decided to sell his house. He was going to net approximately $50,000 from the sale of his home, but he had a tax liability in excess of $100,000. The title search revealed that a federal tax lien was in place. The taxpayer could not consummate the sale until the lien was satisfied or removed. Taxpayers generally think that the Revenue Officer will remove the tax lien so that they can obtain at least partial payment. This is not the case. In many instances, the Revenue Officer will insist on full payment. After all, the IRS has the right to seize the property and sell it at any time for partial payment.

One option is for the taxpayer to obtain a bond for the tax and interest due. To be acceptable to the IRS, the bond must provide for the payment of the tax and interest within six months of the date the statute of limitations on collection is due to expire. This option will not work if the taxpayer is considering using the proceeds of the house sale and some other assets to fund an Offer in Compromise and the tax will not be paid in full.

The bond normally works as follows. You pay a fee to a bonding company and the company will issue a bond that meets IRS requirements. Once you make the bond, the company has agreed to be responsible for your tax liability. Usually the bonding company will satisfy itself that you have sufficient assets to attach to cover any of its payments to the IRS on your behalf. In most cases, taxpayers will not have sufficient assets so this is not the most viable option. Once the Revenue Officer receives the bond, he will issue a Certificate of the Release of Lien (see page 109) and the sale of the property can take place.

Most of my clients have taken advantage of requesting a subordination of a tax lien. The IRS will agree to subordinate the lien. You can use this method when you want to take a second mortgage on your property to pay off the tax liability but the bank will not give you the financing requested because of the federal tax lien. The IRS has the power to release the lien or subordinate the lien if you will pay an amount equal to the lien or the IRS will ultimately collect more money by subordinating the lien and the collection of the tax liability will be enhanced. The IRS requires that you submit an application for a Certificate of Subordination (see page 111). IRS Publication 784 describes how to go about getting a subordination of a federal tax lien. The application must be in writing and provide the following information:

1. Your name and address.

2. Whether the subordination is being made because the IRS will be paid an amount equal to the federal tax lien or because the subordination will facilitate the collection of tax.

3. A detailed description of the property that is subject to the request for subordination.

4. A copy of the Notice of Federal Tax Lien and a description of the lien and the date and place of filing of each lien.

5. A copy of the documents that will create the debt that is taking priority over the federal tax lien if the subordination takes place. You must also describe the transaction that is taking place.

6. You must provide an estimate of the fair market value of the property.

7. You must state the amount of money which will be paid to the IRS if the subordination is granted.

8. You must submit a written statement why you believe that subordination will facilitate the collection of taxes.

9. Any other relevant information to support your application for subordination.

10. The name and address of your attorney.

11. A penalty of perjury statement.

In other instances, the IRS may release the federal tax lien as to one particular property, if it has adequate security in the other property. This will allow you to sell that property to obtain sales proceeds to satisfy a portion of the tax liability. You must request a Release of the Tax Lien (see page 113). Once you have, the IRS will issue a Release of Federal Tax Lien (see page 114).

Form 668. Notice of Federal Tax Lien.

Form **668**	Department of the Treasury · Internal Revenue Service	
(Rev. July 1987)	**Notice of Federal Tax Lien Under Internal Revenue Laws**	

District	Serial Number	For Optional Use by Recording Office

As provided by sections 6321, 6322, and 6323 of the Internal Revenue Code, notice is given that taxes (including interest and penalties) have been assessed against the following-named taxpayer. Demand for payment of this liability has been made, but it remains unpaid. Therefore, there is a lien in favor of the United States on all property and rights to property belonging to this taxpayer for the amount of these taxes, and additional penalties, interest, and costs that may accrue.

A. TAXPAyer

Name of taxpayer

123 TAX BLVD

Residence

Washington D.C.

IMPORTANT RELEASE INFORMATION–With respect to each assessment listed below, unless notice of lien is refiled by the date given in column (e), this notice shall, on the day following such date, operate as a certificate of release as defined in IRC 6325 (a).

Kind of Tax (a)	Tax Period Ended (b)	Identifying Number (c)	Date of Assessment (d)	Last Day for Refiling (e)	Unpaid Balance of Assessment (f)
Income	1988		1-1-90	1-1-96	17,123

Place of filing

	Total	$ 17,123

This notice was prepared and signed at _____, on this,

the _____ day of _____, 19_____

Signature	Title

(**NOTE:** Certificate of officer authorized by law to take acknowledgements is not essential to the validity of Notice of Federal Tax Lien Rev. Rul. 71-466, 1971-2 C.B. 409.)

Part 1 – To be kept by recording office

Form 668 (Rev. 7-87)

Form 668. Notice of Federal Tax Lien. (cont'd)

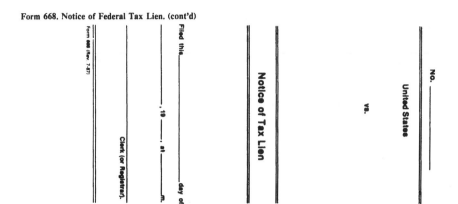

Excerpts From Internal Revenue Code

Sec. 6321. Lien For Taxes.

If any person liable to pay any tax neglects or refuses to pay the same after demand, the amount (including any interest, additional amount, addition to tax, or assessable penalty, together with any costs that may accrue in addition thereto) shall be a lien in favor of the United States upon all property and rights to property, whether real or personal, belonging to such person

Sec. 6322. Period Of Lien.

Unless another date is specifically fixed by law, the lien imposed by section 6321 shall arise at the time the assessment is made and shall continue until the liability for the amount so assessed (or a judgment against the taxpayer arising out of such liability) is satisfied or becomes unenforceable by reason of lapse of time

Sec. 6323. Validity and Priority Against Certain Persons.

(a) **Purchasers, Holders Of Security Interests, Mechanic's Lienors, And Judgment Lien Creditors.**—The lien imposed by section 6321 shall not be valid as against any purchaser, holder of a security interest, mechanic's lienor, or judgment lien creditor until notice thereof which meets the requirements of subsection (f) has been filed by the Secretary

NOTE: See section 6323(b) for protection for certain interests even though notice of lien imposed by section 6321 is filed with respect to

1. Securities
2. Motor vehicles
3. Personal property purchased at retail
4. Personal property purchased in casual sale
5. Personal property subjected to possessory lien
6. Real property tax and special assessment liens
7. Residential property relating to a mechanic's lien for certain repairs and improvements
8. Attorney's liens
9. Certain insurance contracts
10. Passbook loans

(f) **Place For Filing Notice: Form.**—

(1) **Place For Filing**—The notice referred to in subsection (a) shall be filed

(A) Under State Laws —

(i) Real Property — In the case of real property, in one office within the State (or the county or other governmental subdivision), as designated by the laws of such State, in which the property subject to the lien is situated, and

(ii) Personal Property — In the case of personal property, whether tangible or intangible, in one office within the State (or the county, or other governmental subdivision), as designated by the laws of such State, in which the property subject to the lien is situated, or

(B) With Clerk Of District Court-In the office of the clerk of the United States district court for the judicial district in which the property subject to the lien is situated, whenever the State has not by law designated one office which meets the requirements of subparagraph (A), or

(C) With Recorder Of Deeds Of The District of Columbia.—In the office of the Recorder of Deeds of the District of Columbia, if the property subject to the lien is situated in the District of Columbia

(2) Situs Of Property Subject To Lien.—For purposes of paragraphs (1) and (4), property shall be deemed to be situated—

(A) Real Property.—In the case of real property, at its physical location, or

(B) Personal Property —In the case of personal property, whether tangible or intangible, at the residence of the taxpayer at the time the notice of lien is filed For purposes of paragraph (2)(B), the residence of a corporation or partnership shall be deemed to be the place at which the principal executive office of the business is located, and the residence of a taxpayer whose residence is without the United States shall be deemed to be in the District of Columbia

(3) Form —The form and content of the notice referred to in subsection (a) shall be prescribed by the Secretary Such notice shall be valid notwithstanding any other provision of law regarding the form or content of a notice of lien

(g) **Refiling Of Notice.**— For purposes of this section-

(1) **General Rule.**—Unless notice of lien is refiled in the manner prescribed in paragraph (2) during the required refiling period, such notice of lien shall be treated as filed on the date on which it is filed (in accordance with subsection (f)) after the expiration of such refiling period

(2) **Place For Filing.**—A notice of lien refiled during the required refiling period shall be effective only-

(A) if-

(i) such notice of lien is refiled in the office in which the prior notice of lien was filed, and

(ii) in the case of real property, the fact of refiling is entered and recorded in an index to the extent required by subsection (f) (4), and

(B) in any case in which 90 days or more prior to the date of a refiling of notice of lien under subparagraph (A), the Secretary received written information (in the manner prescribed in regulations issued by the Secretary) concerning a change in the taxpayer's residence, if a notice of such lien is also filed in accordance with subsection (f) in the State in which such residence is located

(3) **Required Refiling Period.**—In the case of any notice of lien, the term "required refiling period" means—

(A) the one-year period ending 30 days after the expiration of 6 years after the date of the assessment of the tax, and

(B) the one-year period ending with the expiration of 6 years after the close of the preceding required refiling period for such notice of lien

Sec. 6325. Release Of Lien Or Discharge Of Property.

(a) **Release Of Lien.**—Subject to such regulations as the Secretary may prescribe, the Secretary shall issue a certificate of release of any lien imposed with respect to any internal revenue tax not later than 30 days after the day on which—

(1) Liability Satisfied or Unenforceable - The Secretary finds that the liability for the amount assessed together with all interest in respect thereof, has been fully satisfied or has become legally unenforceable, or

(2) Bond Accepted —There is furnished to the Secretary and accepted by him a bond that is conditioned upon the payment of the amount assessed, together with all interest in respect thereof, within the time prescribed by law (including any extension of such time), and that is in accordance with such requirements relating to terms, conditions, and form of the bond and sureties thereon, as may be specified by such regulations

Sec. 6103. Confidentiality and Disclosure of Returns and Return Information.

(k) **Disclosure of Certain Returns and Return Information For Tax Administration Purposes.**—

(2) Disclosure of amount of outstanding lien - If a notice of lien has been filed pursuant to section 6323(f) the amount of the outstanding obligation secured by such lien may be disclosed to any person who furnishes satisfactory written evidence that he has a right in the property subject to such lien or intends to obtain a right in such property

Form 669-A. Discharge of Federal Tax Lien Under Code Sec. 6325(b)(1).

Form **669-A** (Rev. January 1982)	Department of the Treasury — Internal Revenue Service **Certificate of Discharge of Property from Federal Tax Lien Under Section 6325(b)(1) of the Internal Revenue Code**

Whereas, _A. TAXPAYER_

Of _123 TAX BLVD._ , City of _WASHINGTON D.C._

County of _____ , State of _____

is indebted to the United States for unpaid internal revenue tax in the sum of _17,123.00_

_____ Dollars (\$ _____

lawfully assessed, to wit:

Kind of Tax (a)	Tax Period Ended (b)	Assessment Date (c)	Identifying Number (d)	Unpaid Balance of Assessment (e)
Income	1988	1-1-90		17,123
			Total ▶	\$ 17,123

Whereas, to secure the collection of said tax, notice of the lien of the United States, attaching to all the property and rights to property of the said taxpayer on account of said tax indebtedness, was filed with the _____

_____ for the

_____ , and also with the _____

_____ , in accordance with the applicable provisions of law.

Whereas, the lien of the United States, Federal Number _____ , for said tax has attached to certain

property described as:

Form **669-A** (Rev. 1-82)

Form 669-A. Discharge of Federal Tax Lien Under Code Sec. 6325(b)(1) (cont'd)

(Use this space for continued description of property)

Whereas, the District Director of Internal Revenue has determined that if the certificate of discharge is issued with respect to the foregoing property, the other property which will remain subject to the lien of the United States has a fair market value at this time of at least double the sum of: (1) the amount of the liability remaining unsatisfied in respect of such tax and (2) the amount of all prior liens upon such property;

Now, therefore, this instrument witnesseth, that I, _____ ,

District Director of Internal Revenue at _____, charged by law with the duty of collecting and enforcing the collection of internal revenue taxes due the United States, and charged with the assessment hereinbefore stated, do, pursuant to the provisions of section 6325(b)(1) of the Internal Revenue Code, discharge the property heretofore described from the aforesaid tax lien, saving and reserving, however, the force and effect of said tax lien against and upon all other property or rights to property to which said lien is attached, wheresoever situated.

Witness my hand at _____ , on this,

the _____ day of _____ , 19____ .

Signature	Title

Note. Certificate of officer authorized by law to take acknowledgments is not essential to the validity of Discharge of Federal Tax Lien. G.C.M. 26419, C.B. 1950-1, 125.

GPO 667-181

page 719.198

Form **669-A** (Rev. 1-82)

Form 669-D. Certificate of Subordination of Federal Tax Lien.

Form **669-D** (Rev. August 1983)	Department of the Treasury — Internal Revenue Service **Certificate of Subordination of Federal Tax Lien Under Section 6325(d)(1) of the Internal Revenue Code**

Whereas, _A. Taxpayer_

of _123 Tax Blvd_ , City of _Washington DC_

County of _____ , State of _____

is indebted to the United States for unpaid internal revenue tax in the sum of _17,123.00_

_____ Dollars ($ _____

lawfully assessed, to wit:

Kind of Tax (a)	Tax Period Ended (b)	Assessment Date (c)	Identifying Number (d)	Unpaid Balance of Assessment (e)
Income	1988	1-1-90		17,123
		Total ▶		$ 17,123

Whereas, to secure the collection of said tax, notice of the lien of the United States, attaching to all the property

and rights to property of the said taxpayer on account of said tax indebtedness, was filed with the _____

_____ for the

_____ , and also with the _____

_____ , in accordance with the applicable provisions of law.

Whereas, the lien of the United States, Federal Number _____ , for said tax has attached to certain

property described as:

Form 669-D. Certificate of Subordination of Federal Tax Lien. (cont'd)

(Use this space for continued description of property)

Whereas, the District Director of Internal Revenue has determined that upon the payment of the sum of

_____ dollars *($ _____)* which amount is

equal to the amount with respect to which the tax lien is subordinated and is to be applied in part satisfaction of the

liability in respect of the tax hereinbefore stated which sum has been paid to be so applied, and the receipt of which

sum by me is hereby acknowledged; _____, has authorized the

issuance, under the provisions of section 6325(d)(1) of the Internal Revenue Code, of a certificate subordinating the

tax lien of the United States;

Now, therefore, this instrument witnesseth, that I, _____,

District Director of Internal Revenue at _____, charged by law with the duty

of collecting and enforcing the collection of internal revenue taxes due to the United States, and charged with the

assessment hereinbefore stated, do, pursuant to the provisions of section 6325(d)(1) of the Internal Revenue Code,

subordinate the aforesaid tax lien, in the amount heretofore stated to the instrument herein described as _____

_____

_____,

saving and reserving, however, the force and effect of said tax lien against and upon all other property or rights to

property to which said lien is attached, wherever situated.

Witness my hand at _____, on this,

the _____·_____ day of _____, 19____.

Signature	Title

Note: Certificate of officer authorized by law to take acknowledgments is not essential to the validity of Subordination of Federal Tax Lien
Rev. Rul. 71—466, 1971—2 C.B. 409

Form **669-D** (Rev. 8-83)

Form 668. Notice of Federal Tax Lien. (cont'd)

Form **668** (Rev. July 1987)	Department of the Treasury, Internal Revenue Service **Request for Release of Federal Tax Lien**	
District	**Serial Number**	**Revenue Officer** *(Signature)*
Please release the lien indicated because		**Date**
Account Satisfied *(Date)*	**By: (Cash, M.O., Cert. Check, Personal Check (Not Cert.), Abatement, etc.)**	**Approved** *(Signature of Supervisor/ Manager)*
Statutory Period for Collection Expired *(Date)*	☐ **Bond Accepted**	**Date**
Note: *Requires approval of Chief, Special Procedures function*		
Name of taxpayer A. Taxpayer		**Approved** *(Signature, Chief, Special Procedures function, if applicable)*
Residence 123 Tax Blvd, Washington DC		**Date**

IMPORTANT RELEASE INFORMATION—With respect to each assessment listed below, unless notice of lien is refiled by the date given in column (e), this notice shall, on the day following such date, operate as a certificate of release as defined in IRC 6325 (a).

Kind of Tax (a)	Tax Period Ended (b)	Identifying Number (c)	Date of Assessment (d)	Last Day for Refiling (e)	Unpaid Balance of Assessment (f)
Income	1988	1-1-90			17,123

Place of filing

			Total	$ 17,123

This notice was prepared and signed at _____, on this,

the _____ day of _____, 19____

	Date Filed	Recorder Reference	Recording Fee	Release Fee

Signature _____ **Title** _____

(NOTE: *Certificate of officer authorized by law to take acknowledgements is not essential to the validity of Notice of Federal Tax Lien Rev. Rul. 71-466, 1971-2 C.B. 409.)*

Part 7 – TDA Copy (see over)

Form 668 (Rev. 7-87)

10/11/88 page 719,166G

Form 668. Notice of Federal Tax Lien. (cont'd)

Form **668** (Rev. July 1987)	Department of the Treasury · Internal Revenue Service **Certificate of Release of Federal Tax Lien**	
District	Serial Number	For Optional Use by Recording Offi

I certify that as to the following-named taxpayer, the requirements of section 6325(a) of the Internal Revenue Code have been satisfied for the taxes listed below and for all statutory additions. Therefore, the lien provided by Code section 6321 for these taxes and additions has been released. The proper officer in the office where the notice of internal revenue tax lien was filed on_____, 19_____, is authorized to note the books to show the release of this lien for these taxes and additions.

Name of taxpayer

A. Taxpayer

Residence

123 Tax Blvd, Washington DC

Kind of Tax (a)	Tax Period Ended (b)	Identifying Number (c)	Date of Assessment (d)	Last Day for Refiling (e)	Unpaid Balance of Assessment (f)
Income	*1988*	*1-1-90*			*17,123*

Place of filing

		Total	$ *17,123*

This certificate was prepared and signed at_____, on this,

the_____ day of _____, 19_____

Signature	Title

(**NOTE:** *Certificate of officer authorized by law to take acknowledgements is not essential to the validity of Notice of Federal Tax Lien Rev. Rul. 71-466, 1971-2 C.B. 409.*)

Part 4 – To be kept by SPF

Form 668 (Rev. 7-87)

10/11/88 page 719,166C

If the Period for Collecting Taxes Has Expired, the Federal Tax Lien Should Be Released and the IRS Can No Longer Collect the Tax.

If the IRS has made the assessment in a timely manner, it has six years to collect the taxes after the assessment. Normally the IRS will attempt to collect voluntarily from taxpayer or by levy. Once the period for collection of taxes has expired, the tax is no longer collectable. The IRS is required to release the federal tax lien when the tax liability is paid in full or has become legally unenforceable. IRS Publication 783 provides the procedures for taxpayers to request the release of federal tax liens. In my experience, the IRS does not normally release the federal tax lien without a request from the taxpayer. In most cases the taxpayer has long satisfied the liability and they will hire me to get the lien released.

Beware of the IRS Levy. If You Are Subject to Levy, Get it Released.

The IRS has the most effective enforcement tool. It is called the **levy** (see pages 118–123). It is the way that the IRS can seize your bank account or attach your wages. Your wages and bank accounts are not exempt from levy and the IRS usually wastes no time in attaching wages. If you are levied, you may apply for a release of the property subject to the levy by contacting either ACS or the Revenue Officer who placed the levy. The IRS must release the levy for hardship using Form 911 (see pages 134–137). If the Revenue Officer and ACS will not give you relief, you can apply to the Problem Resolution for immediate release for hardship. You must file a request as soon as possible. This request should outline the hardship you will endure as a result of the levy. If the IRS levies your bank account or your wages, this is easy to prove. You need only show that you need the assets for normal daily living expenses such as food or rent.

Some property is exempt from levy:

◊ Clothes and books.

◊ Furniture, fuel and food up to a set amount.

◊ Books or tools of the trade up to a set amount.

◊ Unemployment compensation.

◊ Mail.

◊ Certain annuity or pension payments.

◊ Workmen's Compensation.

◊ Child support.

◊ A small amount of your wages, salary or other compensation.

◊ Service connected disability benefits.

◊ Public Assistance or Welfare benefits.

◊ Your principal residence, unless the tax is in jeopardy.

The best strategy is to try to avoid being levied in the first place. If you receive a Notice of Intent to Levy from the IRS you should immediately write a letter explaining that the use of liens and levies should be avoided as you are working out a plan to satisfy your tax liability. In your correspondence you should state that you do not currently have the funds to pay the liability in full and that you do not have enough assets to satisfy the IRS. You can also state that your income and expenses are such that you can not afford to have your wages levied or pay large regular monthly installment payments. You should request that ACS put you on a monthly installment payment plan for a small sum of money that you can afford to pay regularly. This should allow ACS to place a hold on collection of your account. The case will shortly thereafter be transferred to a field office.

Form 668-A(C). Notice of Levy.

Form 668-A(C) (Rev. July 1989)	Department of the Treasury-Internal Revenue Service **Notice of Levy**		
Date	District:	Telephone number of IRS Office	

Name and Address of Taxpayer

TO: A. Taxpayer
123 Tax Blvd
Washington D.C.

Identifying Number(s)

Kind of Tax	Tax Period Ended	Unpaid Balance of Assessment	Statutory Additions	Total
Income	1988	17,123	1,000	18,123

THIS LEVY WILL NOT ATTACH TO ANY INDIVIDUAL RETIREMENT ACCOUNT (IRA), RETIREMENT PLAN BENEFITTING SELF-EMPLOYED INDIVIDUALS, OR ANY OTHER QUALIFIED PLAN IN YOUR POSSESSION OR CONTROL.	Total amount due ▶	18,123

Interest and late payment penalty have been figured to _____.

Chapter 64 of the Internal Revenue Code provides a lien for the above tax and statutory additions. Notice and demand, as required by the Internal Revenue Code, have been made, and the taxpayer has neglected or refused to pay. This amount is still due, owing, and unpaid. All property, rights to property, money, credits, and bank deposits now in your possession and belonging to this taxpayer (or for which you are obligated) and all money or other obligations you owe this taxpayer, are levied upon for payment of the tax, plus all additions provided by law. Demand is made on you either to pay this tax liability or pay any smaller amount that you owe this taxpayer.

Money on deposit at banks, credit unions, savings and loans, and similar institutions described in section 408(n) of the Internal Revenue Code must be held for 21 days from the day you receive this levy before it is sent to us along with any interest the taxpayer will earn during that time. In all other cases, you must turn over the taxpayer's property, money, credits, etc. just as though the taxpayer had demanded it.

Please make your check or money order payable to the Internal Revenue Service. Write on your payment the taxpayer's name, the identifying number(s), kind of tax, and tax period shown above, and the words "LEVY PROCEEDS". **Complete the back of Part 2 of this form and mail it to us with your payment in the enclosed envelope.** Keep Part 1 for your records and give Part 3 to the taxpayer within 2 work days. **If you do not owe funds to this taxpayer, please complete the back of Part 2 and return all copies in the enclosed envelope.** Make reasonable efforts to identify all accounts in the taxpayer's name using Address, Social Security, and/or Employer ID number as a minimum. Do not offset funds the Taxpayer owes you without contacting the IRS Office shown above by phone for instructions.

Signature of Service Representative	Title

Part 1 - ADDRESSEE'S COPY

FORM 668-A(C) (Rev. 7/89)

8/15/89 page 719,173

Form 668-A(C). Notice of Levy. (cont'd)

Excerpts from the Internal Revenue Code

★   ★   ★   ★   ★   ★   ★   ★   ★   ★

SEC. 6331.   LEVY AND DISTRAINT.

(b)   Seizure and Sale of Property —The term "levy" as used in this title includes the power of distraint and seizure by any means. Except as otherwise provided in subsection (e), a levy shall extend only to property possessed and obligations existing at the time thereof. In any case in which the Secretary may levy upon property or rights to property, he may seize and sell such property or rights to property (whether real or personal, tangible or intangible).

(c)   Successive Seizures —Whenever any property or right to property upon which levy has been made by virtue of subsection (a) is not sufficient to satisfy the claim of the United States for which levy is made, the Secretary may, thereafter, and as often as may be necessary, proceed to levy in like manner upon any other property liable to levy of the person against whom such claim exists, until the amount due from him, together with all expenses, is fully paid.

SEC. 6332.   SURRENDER OF PROPERTY SUBJECT TO LEVY.

(a)   Requirement —Except as otherwise provided in subsections (b) and (c), any person in possession of (or obligated with respect to) property or rights to property subject to levy upon which a levy has been made shall, upon demand of the Secretary, surrender such property or rights (or discharge such obligation) to the Secretary, except such part of the property or rights as is, at the time of such demand, subject to an attachment or execution under any judicial process.

(b)   Special Rule for Life Insurance and Endowment Contracts.

(1)   In general —A levy on an organization with respect to a life insurance or endowment contract issued by such organization shall, without necessity for the surrender of the contract document, constitute a demand by the Secretary for payment of the amount described in paragraph (2) and the exercise of the right of the person against whom the tax is assessed to the advance of such amount. Such organization shall pay over such amount 90 days after service of notice of levy. Such notice shall include a certification by the Secretary that a copy of such notice has been mailed to the person against whom the tax is assessed at his last known address.

(2)   Satisfaction of levy —Such levy shall be deemed to be satisfied if such organization pays over to the Secretary the amount which the person against whom the tax is assessed could have had advanced to him by such organization on the date prescribed in paragraph (1) for the satisfaction of such levy, increased by the amount of any advance (including contractual interest thereon) made to such person on or after the date such organization had actual notice or knowledge (within the meaning of section 6323 (i)(1)) of the existence of the lien with respect to which such levy is made, other than an advance (including contractual interest thereon) made automatically to maintain such contract in force under an agreement entered into before such organization had such notice or knowledge.

(3)   Enforcement proceedings.—The satisfaction of a levy under paragraph (2) shall be without prejudice to any civil action for the enforcement of any lien imposed by this title with respect to such contract.

(c)   Special Rule for Banks —Any bank (as defined in section 408(n)) shall surrender (subject to an attachment or execution under judicial process) any deposits (including interest thereon) in such bank only after 21 days after service of levy.

(d)   Enforcement of Levy.

(1)   Extent of personal liability —Any person who fails or refuses to surrender any property or rights to property, subject to levy, upon demand by the Secretary, shall be liable in his own person and estate to the United States in a sum equal to the value of the property or rights not so surrendered, but not exceeding the amount of taxes for the collection of which such levy has been made, together with costs and interest on such sum at the underpayment rate established under section 6621 from the date of such levy (or, in the case of a levy described in section 6331 (d)(3), from the date such person would otherwise have been obligated to pay over such amounts to the taxpayer). Any amount (other than costs) recovered under this paragraph shall be credited against the tax liability for the collection of which such levy was made.

(2)   Penalty for violation —In addition to the personal liability imposed by paragraph (1), if any person required to surrender such property or rights to property fails or refuses to surrender such property or rights to property without reasonable cause, such person shall be liable for a penalty equal to 50 percent of the amount recoverable under paragraph (1). No part of such penalty shall be credited against the tax liability for the collection of which such levy was made.

(e)   Effect of honoring levy —Any person in possession of (or obligated with respect to) property or rights to property subject to levy upon which a levy has been made who, upon demand by the Secretary, surrenders such property or rights to property (or discharges such obligation) to the Secretary (or who pays a liability under subsection (d) (1)) shall be discharged from any obligation or liability to the delinquent taxpayer and any other person with respect to such property or rights to property arising from such surrender or payment.

SEC. 6333.   PRODUCTION OF BOOKS.

If a levy has been made or is about to be made on any property, or right to property any person having custody or control of any books or records, containing evidence or statements relating to the property or right to property subject to levy, shall, upon demand of the Secretary exhibit such books or records to the Secretary.

SEC. 6334.   PROPERTY EXEMPT FROM LEVY.

(a)   Enumeration —There shall be exempt from levy—

(1)   Wearing apparel and school books —Such items of wearing apparel and such school books as are necessary for the taxpayer or for members of his family;

(2)   Fuel, provisions, furniture, and personal effects.—If the taxpayer is the head of a family, so much of the fuel, provisions, furniture, and personal effects in his household, and of the arms for personal use, livestock, and poultry of the taxpayer, as does not exceed $1,650 ($1,550 in the case of levies issued during 1989) in value;

(3)   Books and tools of a trade, business or profession.—So many of the books and tools necessary for the trade, business, or profession of the taxpayer as do not exceed in the aggregate $1,100 ($1,050 in the case of levies issued during 1989) in value.

(5)   Undelivered mail.—Mail, addressed to any person, which has not been delivered to the addressee.

SEC. 6343.   AUTHORITY TO RELEASE LEVY AND RETURN PROPERTY.

(a)   Release of Levy and Notice of Release.—

(1)   In general.—Under regulations prescribed by the Secretary, the Secretary shall release the levy upon all, or part of, the property or rights to property levied upon and shall promptly notify the person upon whom such levy was made (if any) that such levy has been released if—

(A) the liability for which such levy was made is satisfied or becomes unenforceable by reason of lapse of time,

(B) release of such levy will facilitate the collection of such liability,

(C) the taxpayer has entered into an agreement under section 6159 to satisfy such liability by means of installment payments, unless such agreement provides otherwise,

(D) the Secretary has determined that such levy is creating an economic hardship due to the financial condition of the taxpayer, or

(E) the fair market value of the property exceeds such liability and release of the levy on a part of such property could be made without hindering the collection of such liability.

For purposes of subparagraph (C), the Secretary is not required to release such levy if such release would jeopardize the secured creditor status of the Secretary.

(2)   Expedited determination on certain business property.—In the case of any tangible personal property essential in carrying on the trade or business of the taxpayer, the Secretary shall provide for an expedited determination under paragraph (1) if levy on such tangible personal property would prevent the taxpayer from carrying on such trade or business.

(3)   Subsequent levy.—The release of levy on any property under paragraph (1) shall not prevent any subsequent levy on such property.

(b)   Return of Property.—If the Secretary determines that property has been wrongfully levied upon, it shall be lawful for the Secretary to return—

(1)   The specific property levied upon,

(2)   an amount of money equal to the amount of money levied upon, or

(3)   an amount of money equal to the amount of money received by the United States from a sale of such property.

Property may be returned at any time. An amount equal to the amount of money levied upon or received from such sale may be returned at any time before the expiration of 9 months from the date of such levy. For purposes of paragraph (3), if property is declared purchased by the United States at a sale pursuant to section 6335(e) (relating to manner and conditions of sale), the United States shall be treated as having received an amount of money equal to the minimum price determined pursuant to such section or (if larger) the amount received by the United States from the resale of such property.

★   ★   ★   ★   ★   ★   ★

Applicable Sections of Internal Revenue Code

6321. LIEN FOR TAXES.
6322. PERIOD OF LIEN.
6325. RELEASE OF LIEN OR DISCHARGE OF PROPERTY.
6331. LEVY AND DISTRAINT.
6332. SURRENDER OF PROPERTY SUBJECT TO LEVY.
6333. PRODUCTION OF BOOKS.
6334. PROPERTY EXEMPT FROM LEVY.
6343. AUTHORITY TO RELEASE LEVY AND RETURN PROPERTY.
7426. CIVIL ACTIONS BY PERSONS OTHER THAN TAXPAYERS.
7429. REVIEW OF JEOPARDY LEVY OR ASSESSMENT PROCEDURES.

For more information about this notice, please call the phone number on the front of this form

Form 668-A(C) (Rev. 7-89)

Form 668-B. Levy.

Form **668-B** (Revised July 1989)	Department of the Treasury — Internal Revenue Service **Levy**

Due from	Originating Internal Revenue District *(City and State)*
A. Taxpayer *123 Tax Blvd* *Washington D.C.*	

Kind of Tax	Tax Period Ended	Date of Assessment	Taxpayer Identification Number	Unpaid Balance of Assessment	Statutory Additions	Total
Income	*1988*	*1-1-90*		$ *17,123*	$ *1,000*	$ *18,123*

		Total amount due ▶	$ *18,123*

The amounts shown above are now due, owing, and unpaid to the United States from the above taxpayer for internal revenue taxes. Notice and demand have been made for payment. Chapter 64 of the Internal Revenue Code provides a lien for the above tax and statutory additions. Section 6331 of the Code authorizes collection of taxes by levy on all property or rights to property of a taxpayer, except property that is exempt under Code section 6334. Therefore, under the provisions of Code section 6331, so much of the property or rights to property, either real or personal, as may be necessary to pay the unpaid balance of assessment shown, with additions provided by law, including fees, costs, and expenses of this levy, are levied on to pay the taxes and additions.

Dated at _____ _____, 19_____.
                                 (Place)   *(Date)*

Signature of Revenue Officer	Telephone Number	Date

Concurrence	Signature of Group Manager	Date
	Signature of District Director or Asst. District Director if taxpayer's principal residence is to be seized, unless Collection is in jeopardy	Date

_____ was asked to be present during inventory. _____
        (Taxpayer's Name)   *(Revenue Officer Signature)*

_____ was present at inventory.   ☐ Yes   ☐ No
        (Taxpayer or Taxpayer's Representative's Name)

Part 1 — SPf Seizure File   Form 668-B (Rev. 7-89)
                                                                           8/15/88 page 719,175

Form 668-B. Levy. (cont'd)

Applicable Sections Under The Internal Revenue Code

Sec. 6321. Lien for Taxes
Sec. 6322. Period of Lien
Sec. 6323. Validity and Priority Against Certain Persons
Sec. 6324. Special Liens for Estate and Gift Taxes
Sec. 6325. Release of Lien or Discharge of Property
Sec. 6331. Levy and Distraint
Sec. 6332. Surrender of Property Subject to Levy
Sec. 6334. Property Exempt from Levy
Sec. 6335. Sale of Seized Property
Sec. 6339. Legal Effect of Certificate of Sale of Personal Property and Deed of Real Property
Sec. 6343. Authority to Release Levy and Return Property
Sec. 7429. Review of Jeopardy Levy or Assessment Procedures

Sec. 6331. Levy and Distraint

(a) **Authority of Secretary.**—If any person liable to pay any tax neglects or refuses to pay the same within 10 days after notice and demand, it shall be lawful for the Secretary to collect such tax (and such further sum as shall be sufficient to cover the expenses of the levy) by levy upon all property and rights to property (except such property as is exempt under section 6334) belonging to such person or on which there is a lien provided in this chapter for the payment of such tax. Levy may be made upon the accrued salary or wages of any officer, employee, or elected official, of the United States, the District of Columbia, or any agency or instrumentality of the United States or the District of Columbia, by serving a notice of levy on the employer (as defined in section 3401 (d)) of such officer, employee, or elected official. If the Secretary makes a finding that the collection of such tax is in jeopardy, notice and demand for immediate payment of such tax may be made by the Secretary and, upon failure or refusal to pay such tax, collection thereof by levy shall be lawful without regard to the 10-day period provided in this section.

(b) **Seizure and Sale of Property.**—The term "levy" as used in this title includes the power of distraint and seizure by any means. Except as otherwise provided in subsection (e) a levy shall extend only to property possessed and obligations existing at the time thereof. In any case in which the Secretary may levy upon property or rights to property, he may seize and sell such property or rights to property (whether real or personal, tangible or intangible).

(c) **Successive Seizures.**—Whenever any property or right to property upon which levy has been made by virtue of subsection (a) is not sufficient to satisfy the claim of the United States for which levy is made, the Secretary may, thereafter, and as often as may be necessary, proceed to levy in like manner upon any other property liable to levy of the person against whom such claim exists, until the amount due from him, together with all expenses, is fully paid.

(d) **Continuing Levy On Salary and Wages.**—[Omitted]

(f) **Uneconomical Levy.**—No levy may be made on any property if the amount of the expenses which the Secretary estimates (at the time of levy) would be incurred by the Secretary with respect to the levy and sale of such property exceeds the fair market value of such property at the time of levy.

(g) **Levy on Appearance Date of Summons.**—

(1) **In general.**—No levy may be made on the property of any person on any day on which such person (or officer or employee of such person) is required to appear in response to a summons issued by the Secretary for the purpose of collecting any underpayment of tax.

(2) **No application in case of jeopardy.**—This subsection shall not apply if the Secretary finds that the collection of tax is in jeopardy.

Sec. 6332. Surrender of Property Subject to Levy.

(a) **Requirement.**—Except as otherwise provided in subsections (b) and (c), any person in possession of (or obligated with respect to) property or rights to property subject to levy upon which a levy has been made shall, upon demand of the Secretary, surrender such property or rights (or discharge such obligation) to the Secretary, except such part of the property or rights as is, at the time of such demand, subject to an attachment or execution under any judicial process.

(d) **Enforcement of Levy.**—

(1) **Extent of personal liability.**—Any person who fails or refuses to surrender any property or rights to property, subject to levy, upon demand by the Secretary, shall be liable in his own person and estate to the United States in a sum equal to the value of the property or rights not so surrendered, but not exceeding the amount of taxes for the collection of which such levy has been made, together with costs and interest on such sum at an annual rate established under section 6621 from the date of such levy, (or, in the case of a levy described in section 6331 (d)(3), from the date such person would otherwise have been obligated to pay over such amounts to the taxpayer) Any amount (other than costs) recovered under this paragraph shall be credited against the tax liability for the collection of which such levy was made.

(2) **Penalty for violation.**—In addition to the personal liability imposed by paragraph (1), if any person required to surrender property or rights to property fails or refuses to surrender such property or rights to property without reasonable cause, such person shall be liable for a penalty equal to 50 percent of the amount recoverable under paragraph (1). No part of such penalty shall be credited against the tax liability for the collection of which such levy was made.

(e) **Effect of Honoring Levy.**—Any person in possession of (or obligated with respect to) property or rights to property subject to levy upon which a levy has been made who, upon demand by the Secretary, surrenders such property or rights to property (or discharges such obligation) to the Secretary (or who pays a liability under subsection (d)(1)) shall be discharged from any obligation or liability to the delinquent taxpayer and any other person with respect to such property or rights to property arising from such surrender or payment.

(f) **Person Defined.**—The term "person," as used in subsection (a), includes an officer or employee of a corporation or a member or employee of a partnership, who as such officer, employee, or member is under a duty to surrender the property or rights to property, or to discharge the obligation.

Sec. 6334. Property Exempt from Levy

(a) **Enumeration.**—There shall be exempt from levy—

(1) **Wearing apparel and school books.**—Such items of wearing apparel and such school books as are necessary for the taxpayer or for members of his family;

(2) **Fuel, provisions, furniture, and personal effects.**—If the taxpayer is the head of a family, so much of the fuel, provisions, furniture, and personal effects in his household, and of the arms for personal use, livestock, and poultry of the taxpayer, as does not exceed $1,650 ($1,550 in the case of levies issued during 1989) in value;

(3) **Books and tools of a trade, business or profession.**—So many of the books and tools necessary for the trade, business, or profession of the taxpayer as do not exceed in the aggregate $1,100 ($1,050 in the case of levies issued during 1989) in value.

(5) **Undelivered mail.**—Mail, addressed to any person, which has not been delivered to the addressee.

(13) **Principal residence exempt in absence of certain approval or jeopardy.**—Except to the extent provided in subsection (e), the principal residence of the taxpayer (within the meaning of section 1034).

(e) **Levy Allowed on Principal Residence in Case of Jeopardy or Certain Approval.**—Property described in subsection (a)(13) shall not be exempt from levy if—

(1) a district director or assistant district director of the Internal Revenue Service personally approves (in writing) the levy of such property, or

(2) the Secretary finds that the collection of tax is in jeopardy.

Sec. 6335. Sale of Seized Property

(f) **Right To Request Sale of Seized Property Within 60 Days.**—The owner of any property seized by levy may request that the Secretary sell such property within 60 days after such request (or within such longer period as may be specified by the owner). The Secretary shall comply with such request unless the Secretary determines (and notifies the owner within such period) that such compliance would not be in the best interests of the United States.

Sec. 6343. Authority to Release Levy and Return Property.

(a) **Release of Levy and Notice of Release.**—

(1) **In general.**—Under regulations prescribed by the Secretary, the Secretary shall release the levy upon all, or part of, the property or rights to property levied upon and shall promptly notify the person upon whom such levy was made (if any) that such levy has been released if—

(A) the liability for which such levy was made is satisfied or becomes unenforceable by reason of lapse of time,

(B) release of such levy will facilitate the collection of such liability,

(C) the taxpayer has entered into an agreement under section 6159 to satisfy such liability by means of installment payments, unless such agreement provides otherwise,

(D) the Secretary has determined that such levy is creating an economic hardship due to the financial condition of the taxpayer, or

(E) the fair market value of the property exceeds such liability and release of the levy on a part of such property could be made without hindering the collection of such liability.

For purposes of subparagraph (C), the Secretary is not required to release such levy if such release would jeopardize the secured creditor status of the Secretary.

(2) **Expedited determination on certain business property.**—In the case of any tangible personal property essential in carrying on the trade or business of the taxpayer, the Secretary shall provide for an expedited determination under paragraph (1) if levy on such tangible personal property would prevent the taxpayer from carrying on such trade or business.

(3) **Subsequent levy.**—The release of levy on any property under paragraph (1) shall not prevent any subsequent levy on such property.

Form 668-B (Rev. 7 89)

Form 668-W. Notice of Levy on Wages, Salary, and Other Income.

Form **668-W** (Rev. January 1990)	Department of the Treasury – Internal Revenue Service **Notice of Levy on Wages, Salary, and Other Income**

Date:	District:	Telephone number of IRS Office

TO: ABC Company
123 Main Street
Washington DC
REPLY:

Name and Address of Taxpayer

A. Taxpayer
123 Tax Blvd
Washington D.C.

Identifying Number(s)

Kind of Tax	Tax Period Ended	Unpaid Balance of Assessment	Statutory Additions	Total
Income	1986	17,123	1,000	18,123
			Total amount due ▶	18,123

Interest and late payment penalty have been figured to _____

This is not a bill for taxes you owe. It is a notice of levy used to collect money owed by the person named in the upper right of this form.

As required by the Internal Revenue Code, notice and demand for the above amount were made on the taxpayer, who neglected or refused to pay. The amount is unpaid and still due. Chapter 64 of the Internal Revenue Code provides a lien for the tax and statutory additions. Items levied on to pay this are: (1) all wages and salary for personal services of this taxpayer that you now possess or for which you become obligated, from the date you receive this notice of levy until a release of levy is issued, and (2) other income belonging to this taxpayer that you now possess or for which you are obligated. These wages, salary, and other income are levied on only to the extent that they are not exempt from levy under Code section 6334 as shown in the instructions. Demand is made on you to pay the total amount due. Do not offset funds the taxpayer owes you without contacting the IRS office shown above by phone for instructions.

If no funds are due this taxpayer, please complete the back of Part 3. Attach it as a cover to the rest of this form and return all parts in the enclosed envelope.

If funds are due this taxpayer, please see the back of this page for instructions.

Signature of Service Representative	Title

Part 1—For Employer or Other Addressee

Form **668-W** (Rev. 1 90)

1/2/90 **page 719,195**

Form **668-D** (Rev. May 1991)	Department of the Treasury – Internal Revenue Service **Release of Levy/Release of Property from Levy**

To *ABC Company* *123 Main Street* *Washington DC*	Taxpayer(s) *A Taxpayer* *123 Tax Blvd* *Washington DC*
	Identifying Number(s)

A notice of levy was served on you and demand was made for the surrender of:

[X] all property, rights to property, money, credits and bank deposits of the taxpayer(s) named above, except as provided in 6332(c) of the Internal Revenue Code—"Special Rule For Banks." See the back of this form regarding this exception.

[ ] wages, salary and other income, now owed to or becoming payable to the taxpayer(s) named above.

Please follow the instructions for the box checked below:

Release of Levy

[ ] Under the provisions of Internal Revenue Code section 6343, all property, rights to property, money, credits, and bank deposits of the taxpayer(s) named above are released from the levy.

[ ] Under the provisions of Internal Revenue Code section 6343, all wages, salary and other income now owed to or becoming payable to the taxpayer(s) named above are released from the levy.

Release of Property from Levy

[ ] Under the provisions of Internal Revenue Code section 6343, all property, rights to property, money, credits, and bank deposits greater than $_____ are released from the levy. The levy now attaches only to this amount.

[ ] The last payment we received from you was $_____ dated _____ . The amount the taxpayer still owes is $_____ . When this amount is paid to the Internal Revenue Service, the levy is released. If you sent us a payment after the last payment date shown, subtract that from the amount you send now.

[ ] Under the provisions of Internal Revenue Code section 6343, all wages, salary and other income greater than $_____ each _____ now owed to or becoming payable to the taxpayer(s) named above are released from the levy.

Dated at _____   _____ , 19 _____
                              (Place)   (Date)

Signature	Telephone Number	Title

Part 1 – To Addressee   Cat. No. 20490C   Form **668-D** (Rev. 5-91)

8/11/91 **page 719,185**

If You Can Afford to Pay Your Tax Liability in Full But Need a Period of Time to Do So, Request an Installment Payment Agreement.

The IRS will normally enter into an installment payment agreement if it will facilitate the collection of taxes. The advantage to an installment payment agreement is that the IRS places a hold on the collection of your account and all levies will be released on salaries and wages and property will not be subject to IRS seizure. You should calculate the monthly payment amount so that you can afford to pay it on a regular basis. In my experience, if you request a period of 2 years or less, it will be acceptable by the IRS. I have had agreements accepted for a longer period of time but the negotiations with the IRS on acceptance of the payment plan have been more difficult.

To begin the process, the IRS will require submission of the Form 433A (see pages 126–129) which is the Statement of Financial Condition. The statement contains information on the whereabouts of all your assets and liabilities. It also contains information about your employment and personal information. The last page asks for information about your monthly income and expenses. It is from this information that the IRS evaluates your request for an installment agreement. You must be able to provide proof of all your income and expenses that you incur on a monthly basis. If you can not do so, the IRS will disallow the expenses. If you have not paid the expense because you had no money to do so, the IRS will also ignore this expense. If the expense will expire in six months, such as a car payment, the IRS will also disregard it. The IRS will also disregard certain expenses if they appear to be excessive. Many times, the IRS will reduce the amount claimed for food.

Once you have agreed with the IRS on a monthly installment agreement (see pages 130–131), you must be certain to remain in full compliance on your taxes for future periods. If you do not, the IRS will start the collection process all over again and you will have the problem of getting the agreement back in place. If the IRS does not accept the installment agreement, you will have provided them a road map to the whereabouts of all your assets that allows the IRS to easily seize your assets. You must be sure to monitor the agreement and keep track of the outstanding balance that you owe.

If the IRS rejects your request for an installment agreement you can appeal to the Regional Office of the IRS for reconsideration. After acceptance of the Agreement, every two years the IRS will review your account and the terms of the installment agreement. At that time they may request additional information. During the period that the installment agreement is in effect, the statute of limitations on collection is extended.

Many of my clients have used the monthly installment agreement to their benefit. It controls potential levy action and allows the taxpayer the opportunity to satisfy their liability at their own pace without costly liquidation of assets at a reduced price.

Form **433-A** (Rev. June 1991)	Department of the Treasury — Internal Revenue Service **Collection Information Statement for Individuals**

NOTE: Complete all blocks, except shaded areas. Write "N/A" (not applicable) in those blocks that do not apply.

1. Taxpayer(s) name(s) and address A. Taxpayer 123 Tax Blvd Washington DC. County _____	2. Home phone number (202) 555-5555	3. Marital status Single
	4.a. Taxpayer's social security number	b. Spouse's social security number

Section I.   Employment Information

5. Taxpayer's employer or business (name and address) ABC Company 123 main Street Washington DC	a. How long employed 2yrs	b. Business phone number (202) 555-5550	c. Occupation manager
	d. Number of exemptions claimed on Form W-4 1	e. Paydays 31st	f. (Check appropriate box) ☒ Wage earner ☐ Partner ☐ Sole proprietor
6. Spouse's employer or business (name and address)	a. How long employed	b. Business phone number ( )	c. Occupation
	d. Number of exemptions claimed on Form W-4	e. Paydays	f. (Check appropriate box) ☐ Wage earner ☐ Partner ☐ Sole proprietor

Section II.   Personal Information

7. Name, address and telephone number of next of kin or other reference none	8. Other names or aliases	9. Previous address(es)

10. Age and relationship of dependents living in your household (exclude yourself and spouse)

11. Date of Birth ▶	a. Taxpayer 06/25/54	b. Spouse	12. Latest filed income tax return (tax year)	a. Number of exemptions claimed	b. Adjusted Gross Income

Section III.   General Financial Information

13. Bank accounts (Include Savings & Loans, Credit Unions, IRA and Retirement Plans, Certificates of Deposit, etc.)

Name of Institution	Address	Type of Account	Account No.	Balance
USA Bank	Washington D.C.	Checking	1234567	100.00
			Total (Enter in Item 21) ▶	

Form **433-A** (Rev. 6-91)

Section III - *continued*   General Financial Information

14. Bank charge cards, Credit Unions, Savings and Loans, Lines of credit

Type of Account or Card	Name and Address of Financial Institution	Monthly Payment	Credit Limit	Amount Owed	Credit Available
n/a					
Totals *(Enter in Item 27)* ▶					

15. Safe deposit boxes rented or accessed *(List all locations, box numbers, and contents.)*

n/a

16. Real Property *(Brief description and type of ownership)*	Physical Address
a. n/a	
	County _____
b.	
	County _____
c.	
	County _____

17. Life Insurance *(Name of Company)*	Policy Number	Type	Face Amount	Available Loan Value
n/a				
Total *(Enter in Item 23)* ▶				

18. Securities *(stocks, bonds, mutual funds, money market funds, government securities, etc.)*:

Kind	Quantity or Denomination	Current Value	Where Located	Owner of Record

19. Other information relating to your financial condition. If you check the yes box, please give dates and explain on page 4, Additional Information or Comments:

a. Court proceedings	☐ Yes ☒ No	b. Bankruptcies	☐ Yes ☒ No
c. Repossessions	☐ Yes ☒ No	d. Recent transfer of assets for less than full value	☐ Yes ☒ No
e. Anticipated increase in income	☐ Yes ☒ No	f. Participant or beneficiary to trust, estate, profit sharing, etc.	☐ Yes ☒ No

Form **433-A**   page 2   (Rev. 6-91)

page 718,470 11/6/91

Section IV.   Asset and Liability Analysis

Description	Current Market Value	Liabilities Balance Due	Equity in Asset	Amount of Monthly Payment	Name and Address of Lien/Note Holder/Obligee	Date Pledged	Date of Final Payment
20. Cash	100		100				
21. Bank accounts (from Item 13)							
22. Securities (from Item 18)							
23. Cash or loan value of Insur.							
24. Vehicles (Model, year, license, tag #)							
a. 1984 Bmw	750		750				
b.							
c.							
25. Real property (From Section III, Item 16) a.							
b.							
c.							
26. Other assets							
a. n/a							
b.							
c.							
d.							
e.							
27. Bank revolving credit (from Item 14)							
28. Other Liabilities (Including judgments, notes, and other charge accounts) a.							
b.							
c.							
d.							
e.							
f.							
g.							
29. Federal taxes owed							
30. Totals	850		$ 850	$			

Internal Revenue Service Use Only Below This Line

Financial Verification/Analysis

Item	Date Information or Encumbrance Verified	Date Property Inspected	Estimated Forced Sale Equity
Personal Residence			
Other Real Property			
Vehicles			
Other Personal Property			
State Employment (Husband and Wife)			
Income Tax Return			
Wage Statements (Husband and Wife)			
Sources of Income/Credit (D&B Report)			
Expenses			
Other Assets/Liabilities			

Form 433-A   page 3   (Rev. 6-91)

11/6/91 page 718,471

Section V.   Monthly Income and Expense Analysis

Income			Necessary Living Expenses	
Source	**Gross**	**Net**		
31. Wages/Salaries *(Taxpayer)*	$ 3333	$ 2000	42. Rent *(Do not show mortgage listed in item 25)*	$ 950
32. Wages/Salaries *(Spouse)*			43. Groceries (no. of people __1__)	200
33. Interest - Dividends			44. Allowable installment payments *(IRS use only)*	
34. Net business income *(from Form 433-B)*			45. Utilities (Gas $ 75 Water $ 20	
35. Rental income			Electric $ 55 Phone $ 30)	180
36. Pension *(Taxpayer)*			46. Transportation /maintenance/gas	245
37. Pension *(Spouse)*			47. Insurance (Life $ _____ Health $ 14	
38. Child Support			Home $ _____ Car $ 85)	99
39. Alimony			48. Medical *(Expenses not covered in item 47)*	100
40. Other			49. Estimated tax payments	.
			50. Court ordered payments	
			51. Other expenses *(specify)*	
			clothing/laundry	170
			animal care	10
41. Total Income	$ 3333	$ 2000	52. Total Expenses *(IRS use only)*	
			53. Net difference *(income less necessary living expenses)* *(IRS use only)*	

Certification — Under penalties of perjury, I declare that to the best of my knowledge and belief this statement of assets, liabilities, and other information is true, correct, and complete.

54. Your signature	55. Spouse's signature *(if joint return was filed)*	56. Date
a Taxpayer		

Internal Revenue Service Use Only Below This Line

Explain any difference between Item 53 and the installment agreement payment amount:

Additional information or comments:

Name of originator and IDRS assignment number:	Date

*U.S. Government Printing Office: 1991 — 282-014/43134

Form 433-D. Installment Agreement.

Form **433-D** (Rev. April 1989)	Department of the Treasury — Internal Revenue Service **Installment Agreement**		

Name and address of taxpayer(s)	Social security or employer identification number	Agreement locator number
A Taxpayer 123 Tax Blvd Washington DC	Kinds of taxes *(Form numbers)* 1040	
	Tax periods 1988	Agreement review date
	Amount of tax owed 18,123	

The undersigned agrees that the Federal taxes shown above, plus any interest and penalties provided by law, will be paid as follows:

$ 500 to be paid on 15th and $ 500 to be paid on the 15th of each month thereafter until the liability is paid in full, and also agrees that the above tax installments will be increased or decreased as follows:

Date of increase (or decrease)					
Amount of change	$				
New installment amount	$				

Conditions:
* This agreement is based on your current financial circumstances and is subject to revision or termination if subsequent financial information required by IRS reflects a change in your ability to pay.
* Failure to provide updated financial information when requested by the Service will be reason for termination of this agreement.
* All Federal taxes that become due during the term of this agreement must be paid on time.
* All Federal tax returns that become due during the term of this agreement must be filed on time.
* Any Federal or State refunds that might otherwise be due will be applied to this liability until it is satisfied.
* If the Conditions of this Installment Agreement are not met, it will be terminated and the entire tax liability may be collected by levy on income, bank accounts, or any other assets, or by seizure of property.
* This agreement may be terminated if collection of the tax liability is endangered.
* **This agreement may require managerial approval; you will be notified if it is not approved.**

Additional conditions:			Originator's name, title and IDRS assignment number:
Your signature	Title *(if corporate officer or partner)*	Date	For assistance call:
Spouse's signature *(if joint liability)*		Date	or write:
Agreement examined or approved by *(signature, title, function)*		Date	

General Information

Employer *(Name and address)*		Taxpayer's Telephone Number(s) ▶	*(Home)*
			(Business)

Banks *(Names and addresses)*

Notice of Federal tax lien filing determination *(check one)*		Earliest CSED
☐ Notice of tax lien not required	☐ Notice of tax lien filed	
☐ Notice of tax lien not filed *(Form 3991 attached)*	☐ Notice of tax lien to be filed County/State _____ taxpayer notified	

Part 1 — IRS Office Copy   Form **433-D** (Rev. 4-89)
12/5/89 page 718,501

Form 433-G. Direct Debit Installment Agreement. (cont'd)

Form **433-G** (Rev. February 1990)	Department of the Treasury — Internal Revenue Service # Direct Debit Installment Agreement	Agreement Locator Number

Name and address of taxpayer(s)	Social security or employer identification number
A Taxpayer 123 Tax Blvd Washington DC	
	Kinds of taxes *(Form numbers)* 1040
	Tax periods 1988
County: _____	**Amount of tax owed** 18,123

The undersigned agrees that the Federal taxes shown above, plus any interest and penalties provided by law, will be paid as follows:

$ _500_ paid with this agreement, $ _500_ to be paid on _Jun 15th_ and on the same day of each month thereafter until the liability is paid in full and also agrees that the above tax installment payments will be increased or decreased as follows:

Date of increase/decrease				
Amount of increase/decrease				
New installment agreement amount				

Conditions of this agreement

- This agreement is based on your current financial circumstances and is subject to revision or termination if subsequent financial statements required by IRS reflect a change in your ability to pay.
- This agreement may require managerial approval. If it is not approved, you will be so notified.
- All Federal taxes that become due during the term of this agreement must be paid on time.
- All Federal tax returns that become due during the term of this agreement must be filed on time.
- Any Federal or State refunds that might otherwise be due will be applied to this liability until this liability is satisfied.
- This agreement to make installment payments may be terminated and the entire tax liability may be collected by levy on income, bank accounts, or other assets, or by seizure of property if the conditions of this agreement are not met, or if it is determined that collection of these taxes is in jeopardy.
- I (we) authorize the IRS and the Depository (bank) identified on the attached voided check to deduct payments (debit) from my (c checking account or correct errors on the account. This authorization remains in effect until I (or either of us) notify IRS in writing to stop or until the liability covered by this agreement is satisfied.
- I (we) understand that if the DEPOSITORY is unable to honor IRS's request for payment due to insufficient funds in my (our) account on the payment due date I (we) will be charged a penalty of $15.00 or two percent of the payment request, whichever is greater. If the payment request is for less than $15.00, the penalty is the amount of the request.
- This account is used primarily for personal _____ business _____ transactions *(check one)*

Additional conditions	Originator's name, IDRS assignment number and function
⌐Attach your blank, voided check here.	For assistance call: Or write:

Your signature	Title	Date	
Spouse's signature *(if joint liability)*		Date	Taxpayer's telephone number: (Home):
Agreement examined or approved by *(signature)*		Date	(Business):

Employer *(name & address)*

Banks *(name & address)* and account numbers

Part 1 - IRS Copy   Form **433-G** (Rev. 2-90)

page 718,512 5/22/90

If Your Property is Subject to Levy Action Know Your Rights. The IRS Must Comply With Certain Procedures to Have a Valid Seizure of Your Property.

In my experience, the IRS has seized my clients' business property, automobiles and bank accounts. In almost all of the cases, I have been able to get the property back. There are a number of ways to get the property released. You can apply to have the property released for hardship. This requires you to file a written request (Form 911) with the Problem Resolution Office (pages 134–137). You can call ACS or the Revenue Officer and negotiate an agreement and release of the property. The IRS must seize the property in accordance with certain procedural requirements. If it is not, then the IRS must release it.

To be a valid seizure, the IRS must deliver the Notice of the Seizure (page 138) to the owner of property. The IRS must also deliver the Notice of Sale and it must be publicly announced. The sale is required to take place not less than 10 nor more than 40 days from the date of the Notice of Sale. If the government does not comply with these rules the sale is voidable. The IRS determines the minimum bid price (page 139). If no one offers this price at the auction of the property, the government must purchase the property for this price and the taxpayer's account must be credited with that amount less the cost of the levy and sale. The minimum bid price is normally 80% or more of the forced sale value of the property less encumbrances. Usually this is based on the wholesale price of the property. The funds received from the sale of the property are normally applied to the expenses of the levy and sale and then to any unpaid taxes. Any remainder is paid to the taxpayer. You can redeem the property prior to the sale upon payment of the tax due plus expenses and costs of seizure. In many cases, my clients have been able to redeem property for the minimum bid price and have not had to pay the liability in full.

If the property is jointly owned by the husband and wife, and only one party has a tax liability, the IRS may nevertheless seize the property in order to liquidate one party's interest in the property. Upon the sale of the property, the IRS must compensate the non-debtor spouse for their interest in the property. Accordingly, the IRS may sell jointly owned property but it can not retain all of the proceeds of the sale. Usually the spouse will be entitled to 50% of the proceeds from jointly held property.

Form **911** (Rev. January 1990)	Department of the Treasury — Internal Revenue Service **Application for Taxpayer Assistance Order** *(ATAO)* **to Relieve Hardship**

Note: Filing this application may result in extending the statutory period of limitations. *(See instructions.)*

Section I.   Taxpayer Information

1. Name(s) as shown on tax return A. Taxpayer	2. SSN/EIN 123 - 45 - 6789	3. Spouse's SSN
	4. Tax form 1040	5. Tax period ended 1988
6. Current address *(Number and street, apt. no., rural route)* 123 Tax Blvd,	7. City, town, or post office, state, and zip code Washington DC	
8. Person to contact	9. Telephone number ( )	10. Best time to call

11. Description of problem *(If more space is needed, attach additional sheets.)*
see attachment A

12. Description of significant hardship and relief requested *(If more space is needed, attach additional sheets.)*

13. Signature of taxpayer or Corporate Officer *(See Instructions.)*	14. Date	15. Signature of spouse shown in block 1	16. Date

Section II.   Representative Information *(If applicable)*

17. Name of authorized representative	18. Firm name
19. Street address or P.O. Box	20. City, town or post office, state, and zip code
21. Telephone number ( )	22. Best time to call	23. Centralized Authorization File *(CAF)* number
24. Signature		25. Date

Section III.   (For Internal Revenue Service only)

26. Name of initiating employee	27. ☐ IRS Identified ☐ Taxpayer request	28. Telephone	29. Function	30. Office	31. Date

Cat. No. 16965S   Form **911** (Rev. 1-90)

page 721,710 3/14/91

Form 911.

Instructions

Purpose of form.—You should use Form 911, Application for Taxpayer Assistance Order *(ATAO)* to Relieve Hardship, to apply for a review by the Taxpayer Ombudsman, or his designee, of actions being taken by the Internal Revenue Service. Such application may be made in cases where you are undergoing or about to undergo a significant hardship because of the manner in which the Internal Revenue laws are being administered. This application can not be used to contest the merits of any tax liability. If you disagree with the amount of tax assessed, please see Publication 1, Your Rights As A Taxpayer. While we are reviewing your application, we will take no further enforcement action. We will contact you after our review to advise you of our decision. The Internal Revenue Code requires us to suspend applicable statutory periods of limitation until a decision is made on your request.

Where to file.—This application should be addressed to the Internal Revenue Service, Problem Resolution Office in the district where you live. Call the local Taxpayer Assistance number listed in your telephone directory or 1-800-424-1040 for the address of the Problem Resolution Office in your district. If you live overseas, mail your request to the Assistant Commissioner *(International)*, Internal Revenue Service, Problem Resolution Office, P.O. Box 144817, L'Enfant Plaza Station, Washington, DC 20026-4817.

CAUTION: Requests submitted to the incorrect office may result in delays. We will acknowledge your request within one week of receiving it. If you do not hear from us within 10 days *(15 days for overseas addresses)* of submitting your application, please contact the Problem Resolution Office in the IRS office to which you sent your application.

Section I. Taxpayer Information

1. Name(s) as shown on tax return. Enter your name as it appeared on the tax return for each period you are requesting assistance. If your name has changed since the return was submitted, you should still enter the name as it appeared on your return. If you filed a joint return, enter both names.

2. SSN/EIN. Enter your social security number *(SSN)* or the employer identification number *(EIN)* of the business, corporation, trust, etc., for the name you showed in block 1. If you are married, and the request is for assistance on a problem involving a joint return, enter the social security number in block 2 for the first name listed in block 1.

3. Spouse's SSN. If the problem involves a joint return, enter the social security number for the second name listed in block 1.

4. Tax form. Enter the tax form number of the tax form you filed for which you are requesting assistance. For example, if you are requesting assistance for a problem involving an individual income tax return, enter "1040." If your problem involves more than one tax form, include the information in block 11.

5. Tax period ended. If you are requesting assistance on an annually filed return, enter the calendar year or the ending date of the fiscal year for that return. If the problem concerns a return filed quarterly, enter the ending date of the quarter involved. If the problem involves more than one tax period, include the information in block 11.

6. and 7. Self-explanatory.

8. Person to contact. Enter the name of the person to contact about the problem. In the case of businesses, corporations, trusts, estates, etc., enter the name of a responsible official.

9. Telephone number. Enter the telephone number, including area code, of the person to contact.

10. Self-explanatory.

11. Description of problem. Describe the action(s) being taken *(or not being taken)* by the Internal Revenue Service that are causing you significant hardship. If you know it, include the name of the person, office, telephone number, and/or address of the last contact you had with IRS. Please include a copy of the most recent correspondence, if any, you have had with IRS regarding this problem.

12. Description of significant hardship and relief requested. Describe the significant hardship which is being caused by the Internal Revenue Service's action *(or lack of action)* as outlined in Section I, block 11. Please tell us what kind of relief you are requesting.

13 and 15. Signature(s). In order to suspend applicable statutory periods of limitations, you must sign this form in Section I, block 13 and block 15, if applicable; or your authorized representative, acting in your behalf, must sign in Section II, block 24. If your name has changed from the name that appears in Section I, block 1, sign using your current legal name. If the request is for assistance on a problem involving a joint return, both you and the spouse shown in block 1 must sign this form in order for the statutory period of limitations to be suspended. If one of the taxpayers is no longer living, the taxpayer's spouse or personal representative must sign the form and write "deceased" after the deceased taxpayer's name. If the taxpayer is your dependent child who can not sign this application because of age or other reasons, you may sign your child's name in the space provided followed by the words "By *(your signature)*, parent *(or guardian)* for minor child." If the application is being made for other than an individual taxpayer, a person having authority to sign the return should sign the application. Enter the date the application is signed.

Section II. Representative Information

If you are the taxpayer and you wish to have a representative act in your behalf, your representative must have a power of attorney of tax information authorization on file for the tax form(s) and period(s) involved. Complete Section II, blocks 17 through 23. *(See Form 2848, Power of Attorney and Declaration of Representative and Instructions for more information.)*

If you are an authorized representative and are submitting this request on behalf of the taxpayer identified in Section I, complete blocks 17 through 23. Sign and date this request in block 24 and block 25 and attach a copy of Form 2848, or the power of attorney.

23. Centralized Authorization File *(CAF)* number. Enter the representative's CAF number. The CAF number is the unique number that Internal Revenue Service assigns to a representative after a valid Form 2848 is filed with an IRS office.

(For IRS Use only)		
ATAO code	Date of determination	Statute suspended ☐ No ☐ Yes: _____ days
How received	PRO signature	

U.S. GPO:1990-717-018/22298

Form **911** (Rev. 1-90)

CHERYL R. FRANK, ESQUIRE

1700 K Street, N.W.

Suite 910

Washington, D.C. 20006

Telephone 202-466-4333

Facsimile 202-429-8702

November 19, 1993

Internal Revenue Service
Problem Resolution Office
Attn: Mr. Terry Ritter
G. H. Fallon Federal Building
31 Hopkins Plaza
Baltimore, Md. 21201

                         Re:

Dear Sir or Madam:

     In accordance with your authority under Section 7811(a) of
the Internal Revenue Code of 1986, as amended, to issue a
taxpayer assistance order on behalf of taxpayer, I would like to
request immediate review of the IRS/ACS collection efforts of
levying taxpayer's wages. The levy notice is attached.

     Absent your issuance of the taxpayer assistance order, the
taxpayer will suffer irreparable harm and significant hardship as
a result of the manner in which the Internal Revenue Laws are
being administered by the IRS.

     On October 27, 1993, I was retained by taxpayer to work out
an arrangement with the IRS so he could satisfy his 1985 and 1986
tax liability. On this same day, I forwarded my power of attorney
to the Philadelphia ACS office. I also faxed the power of
attorney the next day. Taxpayer had received a copy of a Notice
of Levy for wages on his employer dated September 30, 1993. I
immediately phoned ACS and asked for a release of the levy for
hardship. Taxpayer's salary is necessary to pay support for
who does not work and his child, as well as his personal
expenses for rent and food and other fixed monthly expenses. The
person I spoke to in ACS told me that the levy could not be
released at that time, but if I submitted either an offer in
compromise or installment agreement, a hold would be placed on
collection of the account and the levy would be released pending

consideration of the offer.

Accordingly, on **November 5, 1993**, I submitted the Form 433 A as requested and a Form 9465 requesting an installment agreement. On November 18th a member of ACS called me and requested additional information about one of taxpayer's assets and he told me that he had received taxpayer's package. On November 19th, I was told by taxpayer's employer that the levy on his wages had not been released. I called ACS and I was told that it would not be released. No reason was given other than that his case had been "around too long". As soon as I was retained I have been in contact with the IRS to resolve this matter. Taxpayer is anxious to resolve this matter, but levying his wages could result in extreme hardship. If he does not pay   alimony and child support she will not be able to have food or a place to live. His mother also needs a supplemental amount each month for her food. Taxpayer needs to pay his rent, utilities and food each month in order to have the necessities to function in his job. His job is necessary to pay off the IRS. There is no doubt that the IRS will collect on this account. Taxpayer wants to satisfy this obligation. Accordingly, I can not understand the approach being taken by ACS in this matter.

I also informed ACS that I wanted to protest the failure to release the levy after I had met their previous conditions for release. It was my understanding that there is normally a hold on collection of the balance due on an account while an agreement is pending. The IRS representative told me that this was not true and notwithstanding my earlier conversations with ACS the terms for release of the levy had been changed as she had the power to do whatever she decided to collect the account. She also told me that filing this protest would not change the situation as she was in control of the case. I know that there must be some procedure to check on the actions of ACS and therefore I am filing this request.

In view of the above, on behalf of the taxpayer I would like to request that you issue a taxpayer assistance order and release the levy on taxpayer's wages at the earliest possible time. I would also like to request that a hold be placed on collection of the account pending the resolution and acceptance of taxpayer's request for an installment agreement.

Thank you in advance for your expeditious response to this matter.

Sincerely,

Cheryl R. Frank

Department of the Treasury
Internal Revenue Service
Form 2433 (Rev. March, 1988)

Notice of Seizure

Serial number

Name and Address A Taxpayer
123 Tax Blvd
Washington DC

Estimated expenses of seizure and sale
$

Under the authority in section 6331 of the Internal Revenue Code, and by virtue of a levy from the District Director of Internal Revenue of the district shown below, I have seized the property below for nonpayment of past due internal revenue taxes.

Due from	Amount	Internal Revenue District *(City and State)*
	$	

Description of property *(Enter inventory value opposite each item of seized property described)*	$ 5,700
1988 Acura	
Total inventory value	$ 5,700

Property located or stored at *(Show address)*	Disposition of Property & Date	Amt. Rec'd.
555 Seizure Lane Washington D.C.	☐ Redeemed prior to sale _ _ _ _ _ _	$
	Released prior to sale	
	☐ Payment agreement *(amount received at time of release)* _ _ _ _ _ _ _ _	$
	☐ U.S. received its interest _ _ _ _ _	$
	☐ No interest *(no equity in property)* _ _	$
	☐ Future collection potential_ _ _ _	$
	☐ Bankruptcy _ _ _ _ _ _ _ _ _ _	$
	☐ Minimum bid not reached _ _ _ _	$
	☐ Other _ _ _ _ _ _ _ _ _ _ _ _	$
	Sale	
	☐ Public auction _ _ _ _ _ _ _ _	$
	☐ Sealed bid _ _ _ _ _ _ _ _ _ _	$
	☐ Declared purchased for U.S. _ _ _	$
	☐ Disposition unnecessary *(cash applied directly to account)*	
Signature of Revenue Officer making seizure	Address	Date
Signature of accompanying employee	Address	Date

Part 6 — SPf Copy

Form **2433** (Rev. 3-88)

page 737,488 5/9/89

Form **4585** (Rev. June 1991)	Department of the Treasury — Internal Revenue Service **Minimum Bid Worksheet**		☒ Initial ☐ Revised

1. Taxpayer's name *(from TDA)*		2. Seizure number 93-205

3. Liability *(including unassessed accrued amounts)*	$ 180,964.75	
4. Estimated expenses of sale *(from Form 2433)*	$ 700.00	**Amount**
5. Property value *(from Form 2433)*		$ 6,000.00
6. Property value reduction *(not to exceed 25%)*	25 %	$ 1,500.00
7. Forced sale value *(Line 5 minus Line 6)*		$ 4,500.00
8. Percentage of forced sale value *(normally 20%)*	20 %	$ 900.00
9. Reduced forced sale value *(Line 7 minus Line 8)*		$ 3,600.00

Prior Claims

10. *(from Form 2434-B; get District Counsel opinion when necessary)*

Name and Address of Claimant	Type of Claim	Date Recorded	Balance Due/Date Verified
NONE			$

11. Total of prior claims ▶	– 0 –
12. MINIMUM BID PRICE *(Line 9 minus Line 11)*	$ 3,600.00

13. Explain how the fair market value was determined.
Revenue Officer estimate was based on NADA book and condition of auto.

14. Remarks *(Explain the basis for the percentage reductions used. For revised minimum bids, explain the reason for the revision.)*

Property value reduction and forced sale value percentages were determined by risks to potential bidders.

15. Revenue Officer's signature *Jackel A. Revenueofficer*		Date 8-17-93
16. Approval signature	Title Group Manager	Date 8-18-93

Part 3—Taxpayer's Copy *[Remove carbon before completing letter on back of Part 3]*   Form **4585** (Rev. 6-91)

If You Can Not Afford to Pay Your Taxes in Full, Consider Filing an Offer in Compromise. Under this Plan You Agree to Pay a Certain Amount in Full Satisfaction of All Outstanding Tax Obligations.

The IRS may accept an amount that is lesser than the taxes owed in full satisfaction of your tax liability. The IRS calls this an Offer in Compromise. Normally you have to specifically request this and make the initial proposal. The purpose of the Offer in Compromise is to provide delinquent taxpayers with a fresh start toward future compliance with tax laws. There are only two reasons that the IRS will accept an Offer in Compromise. There must be doubt as to collectability or doubt as to liability. Under IRS policy, the IRS will accept an Offer in Compromise "when it is unlikely that the tax liability can be collected in full and the amount offered reasonably reflects collection potential." If neither factor is present, the IRS will reject your offer. You have the burden to prove that one of the two grounds for acceptance of the Offer in Compromise exists.

You must submit the Offer in Compromise on Form 656 (see page 144).

If the Offer is based on doubt as to collectability, you must submit Form 433A with the Offer in Compromise. An Offer based on doubt as to liability does not require the financial statements, but the IRS will make an inquiry to determine if this ground is justifiable.

You can use the Offer in Compromise, based on doubt as to liability, in cases where the IRS made an assessment, but you did not challenge it. In submitting an offer of this type you should be specific in showing how the liability is incorrect. This type of Offer should never be used where the court has already ruled on an issue.

Most Offers in Compromise are based on doubt as to collectability. The IRS currently accepts about 43% of all Offers in Compromise, but this varies by region and office. The Revenue Officer in the case makes a determination of the amount of money a person can fund the Offer with based on the Form 433A that you have submitted and other back-up information. The Internal Revenue Manual provides that the "offer must reflect the taxpayer's maximum capacity to pay, i.e., all that can be collected from the taxpayer's equity in assets and income, present and prospective." The IRS will examine the liquidation value of all of your assets to determine how much you can offer. The IRS will use the value of the asset if taxpayer was forced to liquidate on short notice.

The problem with the system is that in many cases I have submitted an offer on behalf of a client, where I have carefully calculated the value of all the available assets. I go to a meeting with the Revenue Officer. At this meeting the Revenue Officer reviews the Form 433A. Usually, the Revenue Officer tells me that he or she agrees with the amount offered, but the Offer must be approved and an investigation must be made to confirm the information of the Form 433A. About 6 months later, I will receive a letter from the IRS that states that the Offer was not acceptable as the IRS believes that taxpayer can fund the Offer with additional assets. At this point I can not begin to guess what additional assets the IRS is talking about. Usually, there is a problem with the way the IRS values assets. If this is the case, it would seem more logical to call taxpayer in to discuss their valuation and agree on some compromise at this time. Instead, the taxpayer must normally file a written appeal and appear at a hearing at the Regional Office if they decide to protest the IRS action. This is costly and time-consuming for the taxpayer.

In submitting the Offer in Compromise, I normally submit a statement that explains how I arrived at the asset values of the properties. I will also discuss the taxpayer's income and expense requirements to show why an installment agreement is not appropriate. The IRS will consider the amounts that can be collected from taxpayers' future income. The higher the income of a taxpayer, the more difficult it is to get an offer accepted. Other important factors that the IRS considers, are the taxpayer's age and health and future income potential. The older a taxpayer is, the easier it is to get an offer accepted. Any health problems that make future income sporadic are also important to call to the attention of the Revenue Officer. Finally, it is important to remember that the purpose of the Offer in Compromise is to negotiate an agreement so that the taxpayer can once again be in voluntary compliance and be a member of the taxpaying public.

The majority of cases that have used an Offer in Compromise effectively have been non-filer cases. Normally, taxpayer comes to me and has not filed tax returns for a number of years. The tax liability is substantial because the interest and penalties double the amount due. Taxpayer can never reduce his liability through an installment agreement because the interest is accruing faster than monthly installment payments could reduce the tax in issue. Taxpayer is elderly or sick or has severe financial problems in his business or profession so it is not likely that taxpayer's financial situation will improve. In these cases, bankruptcy is not an answer, so there is no other alternative.

In filing the Form 433A you should note the following:

◊ Your net worth (the amount shown on line 27, column (d) of the Form 433A) should equal or be less than the amount offered on the Form 656. If it is not, the Offer will not be processed.

◊ If you have a 401K or IRA, the value should be reduced by tax and penalties for early withdrawal. If you are required to contribute a percentage of your earnings to a pension plan, but you can not withdraw it until separation, retirement or death, the asset will have no value. If the plan is a voluntary plan and the employee can elect to make contributions, the equity shall be the gross amount in the plan reduced by employer contributions. The IRS will evaluate what borrowing potential you have in the plan.

◊ If you have a house, the value should be based on the forced sale value less expenses of the sale. You should obtain an appraisal on this basis.

◊ Your monthly expenses and income should be equal and you must be prepared to verify them. If income exceeds expenses, an installment agreement may be more appropriate.

Acceptance of the Offer in Compromise will require taxpayer to comply with all paying and filing requirements for the following 5 years. No abatements or release of Federal Tax Liens will be made until the total amount offered is paid. Upon submission of the offer, the taxpayer waives his or her right to certain refunds or credit from prior tax years through the year the offer is accepted.

Collection activity on your account will be on hold if it is determined that the Offer merits consideration and there is no reason to believe that collection of the tax will be jeopardized.

The IRS has publicized the Offer in Compromise program as an amnesty program. Unfortunately, it is not.

Department of the Treasury — Internal Revenue Service	▶ File in Duplicate

Form **656**
(Rev. September 1990)

Offer in Compromise

▶ See Instructions
Page 4

Names and Address of Taxpayers

A. Taxpayer
123 Tax Blvd
Washington D.C.

For Official Use Only

Offer is *(Check applicable box)*

☐ Cash *(Paid in full)*

☐ Deferred payment

Serial Number

(Cashier's stamp)

Social Security Number

123-45-6789

Employer Identification Number

To: Commissioner of Internal Revenue Service

Date

Amount Paid
$

1. This offer is submitted by the undersigned proponents (persons making this offer) to compromise a liability resulting from alleged violations of law or failure

to pay an Internal Revenue liability as follows: _1988 income tax liability, interest, penalties_
(State specifically the alleged violation involved, the kind of unpaid tax liability, and each period involved)

2. The total sum of $ _1000_ paid in full or payable on a deferred payment basis as follows: _Within 90 days acceptance of this offer. Funds will be borrowed from friends_

with interest at the annual rate as established under Section 6621(a) of the Internal Revenue Code (subject to adjustments as provided by Code Section 6621(b) and compounded under Code section 6622(a)) on the deferred payments, if any, from the date the offer is accepted until it is paid in full, is voluntarily tendered with this offer with the request that it be accepted to compromise the liability described above, and any statutory additions to this liability.

3. In making this offer, and as a part of the consideration, it is agreed (a) that the United States shall keep all payments and other credits made to the accounts for the periods covered by this offer, and (b) that the United States shall keep any and all amounts to which the taxpayer-proponents may be entitled under the Internal Revenue laws, due through overpayments of any tax or other liability, including interest and penalties, for periods ending before or within or as of the end of the calendar year in which this offer is accepted (and which are not in excess of the difference between the liability sought to be compromised and the amount offered). Any such refund received after this offer is filed will be returned immediately.

4. It is also agreed that payments made under the terms of this offer shall be applied first to tax and penalty, in that order, due for the earliest taxable period, then to tax and penalty, in that order, for each succeeding taxable period with no amount to be allocated to interest until the liabilities for taxes and penalties for all taxable periods sought to be compromised have been satisfied.

5. It is further agreed that upon notice to the taxpayers of the acceptance of this offer, the taxpayers shall have no right to contest in court or otherwise the amount of the liability sought to be compromised; and that if this is a deferred payment offer and there is a default in payment of any installment of principal or interest due under its terms, the United States, at the option of the Commissioner of Internal Revenue or a delegated official, may (a) proceed immediately by suit to collect the entire unpaid balance of the offer; or (b) proceed immediately by suit to collect as liquidated damages an amount equal to the liability sought to be compromised, minus any deposits already received under the terms of the offer, with interest on the unpaid balance at the annual rate as established under section 6621(a) of the Internal Revenue Code (subject to adjustments as provided by Code section 6621(b) and compounded under Code section 6622(a) from the date of default; or (c) disregard the amount of the offer and apply all amounts previously deposited under the offer against the amount of the liability sought to be compromised and, without further notice of any kind, assess and collect by levy or suit the balance of the liability, the right of appeal to the United States Tax Court and the restrictions against assessment and collection being waived upon acceptance of this offer.

6. The taxpayer-proponents waive the benefit of any statute of limitations applicable to the assessment and collection of the liability sought to be compromised, and agree to the suspension of the running of the statutory period of limitations on assessment and collection for the period during which this offer is pending, or the period during which any installment remains unpaid, and for 1 year thereafter. For these purposes, the offer shall be deemed pending from the date of acceptance of the waiver of the statutory period of limitations by an authorized Internal Revenue Service official, until the date on which the offer is formally, in writing, accepted, withdrawn, or rejected. The offer shall also be deemed pending if an appeal is filed with respect to such offer, until the date on which the offer is formally accepted or rejected by the Appeals Office. If a protest is not made within thirty days from being notified of your right to do so, the taxpayer-proponents agree to waive their rights to a hearing before the Appeals Office for this offer in compromise.

7. The following facts and reasons are submitted as grounds for acceptance of this offer: _Doubt as to Collectability_

(If space is insufficient, please attach a supporting statement)

8. It is understood that this offer will be considered and acted upon in due course and that it does not relieve the taxpayers from the liability sought to be compromised unless and until the offer is accepted in writing by the Commissioner or a delegated official, and there has been full compliance with the terms of the offer.

I accept the waiver of statutory period of limitations for the Internal Revenue Service.	Under penalties of perjury, I declare that I have examined this offer, including accompanying schedules and statements, and to the best of my knowledge and belief, it is true, correct and complete.
Signature of authorized Internal Revenue Service Official	Signature of Taxpayer-proponent
Title	Date	Signature of Taxpayer-proponent

Form **656** (Rev. 9-90)

Form 656.

 Department of the Treasury
Internal Revenue Service

Form 656, Offer in Compromise

(Rev. September 1990)

Instructions

Background

Section 7122 of the Internal Revenue Code provides that the Secretary may compromise any civil or criminal case arising under the Internal Revenue laws prior to reference to the Department of Justice. The Commissioner of Internal Revenue has the authority to compromise all taxes not in suit *(including any interest, penalty, additional amount or addition to tax)* arising under the Internal Revenue laws except those relating to alcohol, tobacco, and firearms. This acceptance authority has been redelegated to certain Service officials depending on the jurisdiction of the case and the amount of the liability.

Basis For Compromise

The compromise of a tax liability can only rest on one or both of two grounds—

(1) doubt as to liability for the amount owed,
(2) doubt as to the collectibility of the full amount of tax, penalty and interest owed.

Section 7122 of the Internal Revenue Code does not confer authority to compromise tax, interest or penalty where the liability is determined by the courts and/or there is no doubt as to the ability of the Government to collect. In addition, the Service will not compromise, based on doubt as to liability, any penalty for failure to file information returns, failure to deposit taxes, or tendering bad checks. The doubt as to liability for the amount owed must be supported by evidence, and the amount acceptable will depend on the degree of doubt found in the particular case.

In the case of inability to pay, the amount offered must:

(1) exceed the total value of your equity in all your assets,
(2) give sufficient consideration to your present and future earning capacity, and
(3) you also must be in compliance with all paying and filing requirements for periods not included in the offer. This includes estimated payments, federal tax deposits, etc.

If your offer is acceptable we may require in addition to the above:

(1) a written collateral agreement to pay a percentage of future earnings as part of the offer,
(2) a written collateral agreement to relinquish certain present or potential tax benefits.

In the case of employment tax liabilities of an employer still in the same business as when the liability sought to be compromised was incurred, we will not accept your offer unless:

(1) it is equal to the unpaid tax liability, exclusive of penalties and interest,
(2) your financial condition is such that no greater amount can be collected, and
(3) your current taxes are being paid by deposits as required.

Page 4

Submission of an offer does not automatically suspend collection of an account. If there is any indication that the filing of the offer is solely for the purpose of delaying collection of the tax or that delay would negatively affect collection of the tax, we will continue collection efforts.

Interest and penalties will continue to accrue on the liability while your offer is under consideration. If your offer is accepted and all terms of the offer are satisfied *(i.e., the offer and all collateral agreements are paid in full)* we will abate the balance of the assessment. Please note: Interest will be due at the annual rate, as established under IRC section 6621(a), on any deferred portion of the offer from the date of notice of acceptance until it is paid in full.

Specific Instructions

1) Form 656, Offer in Compromise, must be used if you wish to submit an offer in compromise. The form should be prepared in duplicate and filed in any office of the Internal Revenue Service or directly to the Service Center servicing your area.

Form 433, Statement of Financial Condition and Other Information, must accompany Form 656 if the offer is based on doubt as to collectibility. Form 433 may be obtained at any IRS office. It is your responsibility to obtain Form 433 and fill it out completely so that we may adequately consider your offer.

2) Your full name, address, social security number and/or employer identification number should be entered on the front of Form 656. If this is a joint *(husband and wife)* liability and both wish to make an offer, one offer containing both names may be submitted. However, for any other joint liability, such as a partnership, separate offers must be submitted.

3) You should date the offer on the top of Form 656 in the space provided. This date is important for identification and reference purposes.

4) In item 1, you must list all unpaid tax liabilities sought to be compromised, regardless of type of tax. If you are singly liable *(e.g., employment taxes)* and also jointly liable *(e.g., income taxes)*, separate tax entities exist and separate offers must be submitted. The type of tax and period involved must be specifically identified. Examples of the most common liabilities involved and the proper identification follows:

Wrong	Right	
.1040	Income tax plus statutory additions for the year(s) 19xx . . .	
.941	Withholding and Federal Insurance Contributions Act taxes plus statutory additions for the period(s) ended 9/30/xx, 12/31/xx . . .	
.940	Federal Unemployment Tax Act taxes plus statutory additions for year(s) 19xx . . .	
.100% penalty	100% penalty assessment plus statutory additions incurred as responsible person of Y Corporation for failure to pay withholding and Federal Insurance Contributions Act taxes for the periods ended 9/30/xx, 12/31/xx . . .	

Failure to file penalty	Penalty for failure to file income tax returns plus statutory addition for tax year(s) 19xx. *(Note: This is necessary only if it is a separate offer submitted to compromise a penalty based on doubt as to liability.)*

5) In item 2, the total amount offered should be entered. If the offer is paid in full *(i.e., the total amount is deposited with the offer)* no other entry is required. If this is a deferred payment offer *(i.e., any part of the offer is paid either on notice of acceptance or at any later date)* you should show:

(a) the amount deposited at the time of filing this offer,
(b) any amount deposited on prior offers which are applied on this offer, and
(c) the amount of each deferred payment and the date on which each payment is to be made.

Example. $10,000 paid with the offer and balance of $25,000 to be paid at the rate of $5,000 per month beginning on the 15th day of the month following notice of acceptance and on the 15th day of each month thereafter.

The offer should be liquidated in the shortest time possible, and in no event will the payments extend more than six years. Interest is due at the prevailing Internal Revenue Code rate for any installment(s) due from the date of acceptance to the date of the full payment of the offer.

Amounts deposited with an offer shall be refunded if the offer is rejected or withdrawn, unless a Form 3040, Authorization to Apply Offer in Compromise Deposit to Liability has been executed.

6) In item 7, you must indicate the facts and reasons which are grounds for acceptance of the offer. If the offer is based on doubt as to collectibility, it is normally sufficient to state "I cannot pay these taxes." If your offer is based on doubt as to liability, then these grounds must be fully and completely explained. It would normally be necessary to attach a supporting statement.

7) Please sign the offer in the lower right hand corner of the form. If you and your spouse seek to compromise a joint income tax liability, both must sign. If the offer is to be signed by a person holding a power of attorney, the authorization must be direct and specific and authorize the representative to enter into a compromise of the specific liability.

8) You should be aware that on the Form 656, there are provisions for a waiver of refunds *(item 3)*, a waiver of the statutory period of limitations for collection *(item 6)* and a waiver of the right to contest the liability after the offer is accepted *(item 5)*. A delegated Service official will sign and date the appropriate block to accept the waiver of the statutory period of limitations for collection.

These instructions are intended only as an overview of the offer process and a guide in preparing Form 656. All forms necessary for filing an offer in compromise, plus additional information regarding the procedure can be obtained at local Internal Revenue Service offices.

SURVIVAL #40 STRATEGY

If All Else Fails Consider Bankruptcy, But Make Sure the Taxes Are Dischargeable.

Many times a Revenue Officer has suggested that my client consider bankruptcy instead of an Offer in Compromise. However, not all taxpayers want to declare bankruptcy.

Originally income tax debts were not dischargeable in bankruptcy. This caused taxpayers to remain personally liable for tax debts even though they had gone through bankruptcy. In 1966, Congress amended the bankruptcy code to allow taxes to be discharged under certain conditions. The purpose of this amendment was to allow individuals with large amounts of debt to get a fresh start and be relieved of their obligations; however, it was not done to allow individuals to avoid paying taxes.

In order to discharge taxes in bankruptcy the following three conditions must be met:

(1) The Three Year Rule   Taxes on or measured by income or gross receipts will not be discharged if the taxes are due for a taxable year within a 3 year period prior to filing for bankruptcy. Therefore, in order for the tax to be dischargeable, it must be for a return that was due, including any extensions, at least 3 years prior to filing bankruptcy. Taxes become dischargeable 3 years after their due date including any extensions filed.

(2) The 240 day Rule   The tax must be assessed for at least 240 days prior to filing a petition in bankruptcy. The assessment date is the date the assessment officer signs an assessment certificate. Any taxes that have been assessed within the 240 day period prior to filing for bankruptcy are not dischargeable.

(3) Assessment   Taxes that are not assessed before filing the petition for bankruptcy, but which are assessable by law or agreement are not dischargeable. This rule refers to taxes that are not yet assessed, such as those pending in a current audit, appeal, or Tax Court cases.

The tax debt is a non priority debt, if it meets the above three conditions. Non priority debts are dischargeable. If any of the three conditions is not met, then the tax debt is considered priority debt that can not be discharged.

If the IRS has perfected its security interest prior to the bankruptcy petition by recording a tax lien, the tax will not be dischargeable. Once the IRS becomes a secured creditor even if the taxes are dischargeable, the lien will survive bankruptcy. A tax lien is only secured to the extent of the value of the property to which it is attached. However, even though the taxing authority's interests may be perfected, bankruptcy may still be a useful tool to reduce tax liability. This is because the bankruptcy court has the authority to determine the amount or legality of any tax, fine, or penalty related to a tax whether or not previously assessed or paid. This gives the bankruptcy court the authority to determine the amount of tax due even though it does not have the authority to discharge the debt.

There are certain taxes that are always priority taxes:

(1) Payroll Taxes.   There are three types of payroll taxes. They include employer FICA, employee FICA withheld, and income tax withholding. The latter two taxes are trust fund taxes because a company is collecting and paying the taxes for someone else. The trust fund taxes are never dischargeable in bankruptcy. Additionally, if not paid, responsible persons may be assessed a 100% penalty. Responsible persons can include corporate officers, directors and shareholders. The 100% penalty holds these individuals personally liable for the taxes. The 100% penalty is not dischargeable in bankruptcy.

(2) Penalties   Ordinarily, penalties are given the same treatment as the related tax. If the tax receives priority treatment and is nondischargeable in bankruptcy, then the penalty will receive the same priority treatment and will be nondischargeable in bankruptcy.

The filing of a bankruptcy also puts an automatic stay on the collection of taxes. The Revenue Officer must stop all wage levies as you are protected from your creditors. The IRS will be prevented from perfecting a tax lien on the debtor's assets, seizing and selling property, or the levying the debtor's property. This allows the debtor the time to organize his financial situation on his own terms without fear of having his affairs arranged by a third party. There is a disadvantage to the automatic stay. The downside is that the statute of limitations on assessing and collecting the tax liabilities is tolled during the automatic stay. The trustee of the bankruptcy estate will step in to negotiate an arrangement with the IRS. In many instances, a forced sale of your assets will be avoided. If you believe you are eligible to use the advantages of bankruptcy in dealing with your tax situation, consult a tax and bankruptcy attorney. Unfortunately, I have seen individuals file bankruptcy prematurely and therefore the time periods have not been satisfied so that the bankruptcy does not discharge the taxes they thought would be discharged.